SEVEN SONGS
IN
SEVEN DAYS

Other CDs by Jane Fallon

Faces (1999)

City Girl (2006)

jane plain (2008)

Gemini Rising In A Patchwork Sky (2010)

www.janefallon.com

This is an early picture of Gerald (Jerry) Dwane Ross.
It was taken after the family moved to California.
He was 13 years old.

It was good days—we had nothing but we had everything. We didn't have a bunch of fancy clothes and such, but they were clean and the holes were patched in 'em and we always had a good dry place to sleep and plenty to eat and that's all you needed. It wasn't a fast life that you lived in those days.

Jerry Ross

SEVEN SONGS IN SEVEN DAYS

JOURNEY OF AN ARKANSAS TRAVELER

JANE ROSS FALLON

DEDICATION

This book is dedicated to my father and mother who did their best to provide their six children with a loving home filled with laughter. It is also dedicated to their pioneer spirit and hard work ethic, which became our example, to their strong religious faith, which became our rock, and to their love of music, which became our light and joy.

ACKNOWLEDGEMENTS

I extend a special thanks to songwriters Bob Franke and Cliff Eberhardt for their songwriting guidance and words of wisdom; to Rick Cooper, Judy Gross, Howie Rashba, Crystal Bickford, Steve Rapson, Terence Hegarty, Tag Vennard, and Jack Fallon Sr. for reading the initial drafts and giving important feedback, and to Camille Breeze for her stylistic suggestions. Thanks to Jerry Ross, JT Ross, Drothey Ross Zgraggen, and Janice Butler Ross for sharing their memories.

In addition, I'd like to thank Gail Stephens, The Exhibit Director at the Old State House History Museum in Little Rock, Arkansas, for her help with "She Appeared To Be 18 or 19 Years Old."

Additional editing and proofreading was provided by Brenda Ayers Hajec, Adjunct Professor of English at Merrimack College, Andover, Massachusetts.

Printed in the United States of America
First Printing 2011

Fallon, Jane
    Seven Songs in Seven Days:
    Journey of An Arkansas Traveler

ISBN-13:
978-0615508733

ISBN-10:
0615508731

For additional copies of this book, or to purchase the accompanying musical CD, please visit:

www.janefallon.com/sevensongs.html

CONTENTS

CONTENTS

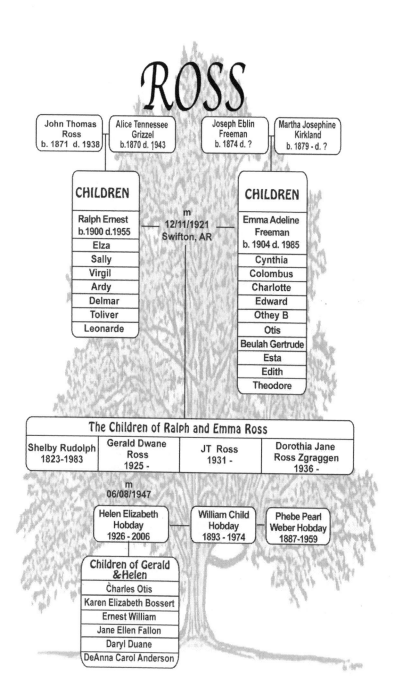

ROSS

| John Thomas Ross b. 1871 d. 1938 | Alice Tennessee Grizzel b.1870 d. 1943 | Joseph Eblin Freeman b. 1874 d. ? | Martha Josephine Kirkland b. 1879 - d. ? |

CHILDREN

Ralph Ernest b.1900 d.1955	
Elza	
Sally	
Virgil	
Ardy	
Delmar	
Toliver	
Leonarde	

m
12/11/1921
Swifton, AR

CHILDREN

Emma Adeline Freeman b. 1904 d. 1985
Cynthia
Colombus
Charlotte
Edward
Othey B
Otis
Beulah Gertrude
Esta
Edith
Theodore

The Children of Ralph and Emma Ross

| Shelby Rudolph 1823-1983 | Gerald Dwane Ross 1925 - | JT Ross 1931 - | Dorothia Jane Ross Zgraggen 1936 - |

m
06/08/1947

| Helen Elizabeth Hobday 1926 - 2006 | William Child Hobday 1893 - 1974 | Phebe Pearl Weber Hobday 1887-1959 |

Children of Gerald & Helen

Charles Otis
Karen Elizabeth Bossert
Ernest William
Jane Ellen Fallon
Daryl Duane
DeAnna Carol Anderson

INTRODUCTION

What would an airport be without the *USA Today*? Comprised of major headlines and short, pointed articles, it seems tailor-made for the scattered attention span of the traveler with one ear cocked toward the loudspeaker. I picked up a paper and scanned it lightly, leaning against the wall at the Seattle airport. I could see that my plane had arrived and figured it would take about 15 minutes to unload the old passengers and line up the new ones.

Nothing caught my attention until I got to the "Lifestyle" section. There I saw an article that described a current trend. It seems that the newest rage in authorship is to do something and then write about it. One man had read the OED (*Old English Dictionary*) and chronicled the entire ordeal. A woman claimed to have had sex with her husband every night for a year and used this experience as inspiration for her stab at literary stardom.

The idea was intriguing (not that last idea but the concept itself!) and as I boarded my plane, I began thinking about what I might do to write about. Something came to me at once: I could probably write a song a day.

Immediately some little ditty about the *USA Today* entered my head. It was frivolous and bouncy with too much rhyme and went nowhere, but the idea lingered and would not be dismissed. How long could I do it, I wondered? I had only one week left on the West coast before I had to return to New England, so I decided to focus on that week. I would be staying with my Dad in Bonanza, Oregon, and I had plans to travel a bit around the state with him. I figured that given the movement from place to place, I could find inspiration.

Very early in the process, probably day two, I realized that there was so very much more to this than I had at first thought. As I listened to my dad talk, as he shared his stories, I felt that the songs and the stories began to merge. I wanted to tell these stories. My original seven songs idea became part travelogue, part biography, and part creative treatise. When the week was over, and I went home with six of my seven songs, the premise continued to haunt me. I had begun the search for my roots through my father.

And so what had started as a one-song-a-day challenge opened like a flower, the petals expanding, each becoming laden with journeys and stories and music. *Seven Songs in Seven Days* gained the sub-title of Journey of an Arkansas Traveler.

The songs, the stories, the journey all became one. Dad's memories brought back my memories. All were bound together by music, which is where my roots lie and is a conduit through which I remember.

My dad, Gerald (Jerry) Dwane Ross, left Arkansas as an 11-year-old with his mother, father, two brothers, a sister, and three cousins and joined the great migration from the Southern states to California on Route 66, the road that became known as The California Road. It was 1936, and the Great Depression had taken its toll across the South. His family made the westward march from guaranteed poverty to potential prosperity.

This book is a journey of self-discovery — a journey to find a sense of place, to reveal what I can of a special generation for whom work was just "what you did" and to a time when life was less complicated than it is now. Mostly, however, this journey brings me home. It brings me to a home that expands far beyond the limits of a house or a country and into the realm of the soul and spirit.

My friend Mary Pratt, a lovely singer-songwriter with whom I share time at a songwriting-critique session once a month, suggested that I write an introductory song to this series and so I did. I used it to publicize the live recording I was doing and to invite people to join me there. And now, I use it to invite the reader to join me as well.

Come and Journey with Me

There is meaning in this life that must be spoken.
There are tales that with their magic set us free.
Blessings are in hand with each turning of the sand
as we walk across this land.
Come and journey with me.
Wind out of the desert seems to whisper
as it drifts into the mountains
and jumps from tree to tree.
Like the turning of a page speaking wisdom born of age
we recount at every stage.
Come and journey with me.
Life is a river, pulling us along.
It is cool and dark and deep, as melodious as song.
We travel on our journey; we are walking side by side.
Let us pull back from the shadows
where the sweetest stories hide.
There is weight in this world that we must carry.
There is happiness and mirth, there is pain and misery.
As we wander we will find people brave and kind
who stay with us in our minds.
Come and journey with me.
There's not more I can say, just that I hope and pray
that you'll join me on my way.
Come and journey with me.

This work takes that journey, communicating to others the spirit of another generation, painting pictures with words of places and events— making connections.

PART I

JANUARY 2011

A TRIP TO ARKANSAS

A house stopped in time in Alicia, Arkansas

As I wandered through the town of Alicia, Arkansas, I found an abandoned house; the rusty automobile in front of the dilapidated building indicated a town stopped in time, bypassed by history. My Dad grew up in a sharecropper's shack somewhere in the woods near this town.

Shelby and I used to fish in the crick for crawdads. We'd tie a piece of side meat on a string attached to a willow pole. The crawdads would latch on to it. We'd build a fire and cook 'em up and eat 'em right there.

Jerry Ross

I travel to Alicia in search of a "crick."

A SENSE OF PLACE

That people could come into a world in a place they could not at first name
and had never known before; and that out of a nameless and unknown place
they could grow and move around in it and call it HOME, and put roots
there; so that whenever they left this place they would sing homesick songs
about it . . . remembering the grouping of old trees, the fall of slopes and hills,
the lay of fields and the running of rivers; of animals there, and of objects
lived with; of faces and names of of life and belonging, and forever be
returning to it or leaving it again.

William Goyen, *The House of Breath*

APPROACHING A PLACE I've never been always fills me with a slight
sense of wonder. We live on such a vast, interesting planet, and I am
always amazed by how it is all the same and yet different and so
grateful when I can see another part of it.

I looked down from the airplane as we approached Little Rock,
Arkansas and saw rice fields spreading out in a checkerboard of
greens and tans. This, the birthplace of my dad, was a place that I had
never been.

"I'm going to go to Arkansas." I had made this decision just weeks
earlier and told my husband.

He looked at me reflectively and quietly for a moment. "What
brought that on?"

"Well, I have never been to the state where my dad came from. I am
trying to write this book that will tell some of his stories and I'd like to
try to grasp that time period. I think that maybe by going there I can get
a sense of the place and put his stories into perspective."

How important could this trip be I wondered? Arkansas must have
changed. I assumed that it must be possible to do the same research
online and that physical access to materials wasn't necessary.

But the desire lingered. I asked Crystal Bickford, Director of
Composition at Southern New Hampshire University, where I teach, for
her opinion.

"Oh yes," she said. "I think that's a great idea. And take a camera."
She pointed to various photographs that line her office walls. "You can
see what I do."

I have a friend in Arkansas who lives in the Western part of the state, hours from where I'd be exploring. He pointed out that the Eastern part of the state is much different from the Western part.

"Folks out here call the Eastern part of the state the 51st state; it is that different from the Northwest part."

So perhaps it hadn't changed that much from the Arkansas that my dad knew after all. It was still a rural land, except that rice fields had replaced the cotton fields of his youth.

The airport was small and sleepy and catching the hotel shuttle was easy. I planned to stay right downtown within walking distance of the places I wanted to see the first day: the Old State House, the Capitol, and the municipal library with its genealogical collections. On day two, I planned to rent a car and take a trip out to where my dad was raised, the town of Alicia.

I loved my time in Little Rock. First of all, I loved the name. In 1721, a French explorer sailing down the Arkansas River and landed at a stone outcropping he dubbed "le petite roche." Second, I loved the compact nature of the downtown. I was able to explore the historic district and the state capital on foot. Third, I loved the parks and shops along the river, the historic homes and the subdued, casual atmosphere. After spending most of one afternoon in the Arkansas Studies Institute (ASI —part of the Central Arkansas Library System and dedicated to Arkansas history) and the rest of the day in the Old State House History Museum, I spent the evening cheering for the Arkansas Razorback football team in a local bar.

The next morning I was also able to visit the Capitol building with its vast genealogy wing. Searching through the stacks at the ASI, I found what I believed to be the gravestone of my great grandparents and finding that graveyard became part of the next day's itinerary.

MY THIRD DAY in Arkansas was bright and sunny, and I picked up my car at the Little Rock airport and headed north. The road was moderately traveled, the highway smooth, and the view vast and uncluttered. The Ralph and Emma Ross family lived near Alicia, Arkansas, when my dad was young. Ralph, my grandfather, hired out as a day-laborer, making one dollar a day for pulling weeds and picking some cotton. Emma, my grandmother, and the two oldest boys, Shelby and Gerald, earned about 75 cents a day. In addition, they received free lodging: a small cabin without running water, indoor plumbing, or electricity.

I had no idea what the population might have been in Dad's time; it might have been bigger. Alicia is situated on both a rail line and a river, which should indicate potential prosperity. The town did not look very prosperous. The newest building in town was the post office, and I found one very nicely kept up white, New England style home. Other than that, the buildings were old and run down.

The main drag, also a major thruway, was lined with three unused buildings. One looked as if it might have been a gas station and one was marked with a sign called "antiques." Surely it must have seen better days. The early inhabitants of this land settled here for a reason.

Now, Dad didn't live in the town of Alicia. He remembered that their cabin was in a wooded area somewhere outside of town. I pulled over to the side of the road and called Dad's phone.

"Hey Dad, I'm in Alicia," I said.

"You are! Well how 'bout that."

"The landscape is gray and bare; not much is growing because it's winter, I guess. On either side of the highway there are cleared fields."

"I remember lots of trees surrounded our house," he said.

"Well, I think they've done a lot of clearing since that time. I see trees, but I see more open field. I'm looking for a "crick." One like you and Shelby might have fished in."

He laughed. "Shelby and I had fun fishin' for crawdads, I remember."

"I was in Little Rock all day yesterday and while researching in the library, I think I found out where Grandpa's parents are buried. Was your grandmother known as 'Tennessee?' I found a J.T. Ross and an Alice Tennessee Ross."

"Yep. That would be them. I think Grandpa was Joseph Thomas and I know Grandma was Alice."

"I'll go now Dad and call you once I find the gravestones, OK?"

"OK. Talk to ya later."

The trip to Walnut Ridge took about 20 minutes. Once there, I logged onto the free WIFI in the local McDonald's in order to take a look at a map to find Austin Cemetery. Once known as Old Walnut Ridge Cemetery, it is located one and one half miles north of town, then two and one half miles west, located behind a large red metal building. As I had traveled that morning, I had seen other cemetery markers. It had been tempting to stop at everyone. How interesting it all was, those little graveyards tucked away in the back of the local farms. I was pleased to have found this place; it was so peaceful, isolated, and restful. I took a lot of pictures to show my Dad.

John Thomas and Alice Tennessee (nee Grizzell) Ross are buried in this small, sparse graveyard on a back lot of someone's farm in a cemetery that is now called Austin and is just outside of Walnut Ridge, Arkansas. It took me a while to find the gravestone. Set apart, with no other family near, is a nicely crafted stone with one side bearing the name of J.T. Ross and the other inscribed with the name of Alice Tennessee Ross. Who put the stone there, and when, I do not know but John Thomas died in 1938, just two years after his son and family set forth for a new life.

As I DROVE BACK to Little Rock from Walnut Ridge, I mused over what I had seen. A sense of place—this country was the birthplace of my father and the early cradle where he was nurtured, where he fished in the 'crick' and did his chores and went to church in a country brush arbor. He did not have running water or indoor plumbing but ran in barefoot exuberance through the thickets and plains with a healthy body.

"We had a good life," he told me. "We had everything we might need. A place to sleep, food to eat, good times."

He had a home. He lived in Arkansas and it lives in him. He never quite lost the accent, his Baptist roots, and his penchant for fun and hard work, sometimes not differentiating between the two.

I was his daughter looking for my father there, imagining his clean features and blond hair, his ready laugh and quick wit, helping with the chores, getting into trouble, fishing and fighting with his brothers. I might not have been able to actually see him, but I now had a glimpse into the place that shaped him, the home he had to leave, and the sturdy Arkie roots that were severed by economic necessity and sent drifting toward the California Road.

WHO AM I?

I most likely descend from one of America's most stereotypical and undying folk images: the Southern poor white. This image has long been a point of contention with the region's defenders. They argue that the Southern whites were not lazy indigents or wealthy exploiters but rather solid citizens, plain and sturdy good old boys who worked hard and provided for their families.

I had heard my dad and my aunts mention that my grandmother used to get a little hot under the collar about certain perceptions. "We weren't dirty," she'd say. "There were streams and we'd wash ourselves and our clothing, and I always kept everything mended."

Some folks remember the clotheslines that were strung in great numbers around the tent cities. Many travelers recollect that even though they didn't have a dime, they cleaned up everyday. Cleanliness was, after all, next to godliness, and the women fixed their hair and took pride in their personal appearance. In one Ross family photo, taken as they prepared to embark on their journey, my Grandma

Emma poses in a flowered dress and ladylike hat. On her lap, my aunt Drothey is spotless in white and next to them my uncle JT bears smudges of little-boy dirt, but his overalls and shirt are free from rips and tears and will most likely go into the wash at the next opportunity.

Simple travelers—migrants—the history of the world is filled with them. They are people of strength and character; they believe in God and family and they flee from penury and possible starvation to seek new lives; they reaffirm our faith in the power of the human spirit in the face of adversity.

Because I cannot trace my family any further back than Arkansas, to Great Grandpa Thomas Ross, I assume that my Scottish ancestors emigrated sometime in the 1800's and settled in the hills of the South, eventually finding their way to the more fertile moderation of the lowlands of Arkansas. (Ross is a Scottish name and the Scots who ended up in the South usually emigrated during this period.) Perhaps more assiduous scholarship at the genealogy library could help turn up additional lineage. Somehow I doubt it. My own father is without a birth certificate. He has no knowledge of how the Rosses came to settle in Arkansas, nor did his father. My grandmother's family came to Arkansas from Missouri by covered wagon but no one knows why they left.

The Old State House in Little Rock has been turned into an interesting museum of Arkansas history. A prominent display there features a wide variety of Arkansan lore.

Favorite sons and daughters of this rural state abound. As I wandered through the museum, I was reminded that many Arkansans left their mark on international popular culture: musicians Al Green and Louis Jordan; politicians J.W. Fulbright, Winthrop Rockefeller, and Bill Clinton; athletes Brooks Robinson and Scottie Pippen; movie stars Alan Ladd and Mary Steenburgen. I was also reminded that the election of Bill Clinton to the presidency gave lie to the notion that Arkansas was just a hillbilly state. Brook Blevins, curator at The Old State House Museum said, "We had a Rhodes Scholar, Yale-educated governor, who went on to become a two-term president of the United States."

Well, my dad was no Rhodes scholar, but he is a decent, hardworking man, as was his father before him. He grew up to learn to appreciate the small things and to live with very little and to never complain about it.

For my dad, life was just a simple migration from a home in Arkansas to homes in other places. There in Arkansas, amid the open spaces, trees, and streams, I could envision the Ross family and their friends working hard, laughing, playing, and loving, not as the toothless, lecherous, uneducated hillbillies often depicted in literature and movies but a simple, normal family, decent, spiritual, just doing what had to be done from day to day.

Who I am is not determined by the names and dates of ancestors but rather by this character and this spirit. I could feel it there in Arkansas as I gazed out on the plowed fields, the bird-filled skies, and the small, muddy creeks. A sense of place—home to the man who made a home for me.

THE TRIP HAD worked its magic. I had found "the crick." I was ready . It was all waiting, lying in a heap in my memory, on scraps of paper, and in digital recordings: the story of an Arkansas traveler and seven songs written in seven days on a journey that crossed a continent and spanned three generations, while exploring the realms of inspiration and creativity.

MUSIC . . .

is some kind of electricity

that makes a radio out

of a man and the dial is in his head

and he just sings according to how he's feeling.

The best stuff you can sing about

is what you saw

and if you look hard enough

you can find plenty to sing about.

Woody Guthrie

PART II

JUNE 2008

SEVEN SONGS IN SEVEN DAYS

Jane Ross Fallon, age 20, singing at a friend's wedding.

I cannot remember a time when I did not sing, when I did not make up songs or stories. I cannot remember a time when creativity was not an important part of my existence even in the doll clothes I made or the cakes I baked. I cannot remember a time when family has not been a major focus of my life.

Jane Ross Fallon

Home

Dad was waiting for me at the Klamath Falls, Oregon airport and he was easy to spot, still tall despite the stooped back, his cowboy hat somehow prominent in a place where cowboy hats are not out of place.

"Hi, sis," he said, giving in to my hug.

After collecting my suitcase, we jumped into the old burgundy Pontiac and headed west to his house in Bonanza, Oregon. I have traveled the road many times since my parents moved there, sometimes as a passenger but usually on my own in a car rented at the Portland, Oregon, or Sacramento, California, airports, depending on where I had flown into from the East coast.

I think it lucky that I like to travel, given the direction my life has gone—Western girl gone East. I had made the cross-country journey frequently and after visiting college friends in Portland or relatives in Sacramento, traveled five or six hours to that remote outpost in the Oregon High Desert.

I either left the fertile Willamette Valley and cruised across the high Cascade passes, or headed north from the golden valley of Sacramento and past the imposing snow-covered Mt. Shasta, but either way I would end up in Klamath Falls and head out towards Bonanza, a town of about 450 people, on Highway 140.

This day was different, however. It was one of those times when I arrived at the airport and Dad was there to pick me up. The road to my dad's place stretched out about 45 miles from Klamath Falls, at first fast and flat as it left the town then eventually curling through little valleys and around hills and near a small stream. The openness, a sharp contrast to the lushness of the New England forests, cleared my head, somewhat like a shot of mental menthol, and it was impossible to miss the hawks and eagles that flew low over the fields.

My parents had moved to Bonanza in 1991 when Dad officially retired. The ranch at Silver Lake, Oregon that he had been managing had sold. He was 66 years old but, unlike many men that age, he didn't really want to retire. Cattle ranching had been his life. He loved the toughness of it, the long days, the strenuous work of building fence and making hay, the long, grueling days on horseback, and the camaraderie of men.

My mother, on the other hand, was ready. Like most countrywomen she had done more than her share. She had spent hours fixing up houses that were not her own, rode with the men or worked in the garden, and then headed into the kitchen to prepare a feast for the workers as if by magic. Dad had the possibility of another job at another ranch but Mom said no. It was time to settle someplace of their own and relax the twelve hour workday.

While Dad wrapped up the ranch business, Mom went shopping—for a place and a house. She set her sights on a location near Bonanza, Oregon, where my sister Karen lived. Karen was raising my younger sister DeAnna's children. DeAnna had taken her own life at the age of 23 and left two small children; my mother very much wanted to live near these children of the daughter she had lost.

I've heard my Dad tell the story many times since Mom's death in 2006, marveling at how she did it all by herself. She decided on seven acres, five miles down the road from my sister. There was an old doublewide mobile home on the property, which she replaced with a newer model—$41,000 later, she was a homeowner.

When Dad joined her, his first priority was to build decks around the front and the back of the house. Mom sometimes grumbled about it—not because she didn't like the decks but because her priorities might have been more of the interior cosmetic variety. In the long run, those additions gave the house a stability and permanence, and the aspens grew to a great fringe around the back deck, shading it from the hot western sun.

On my bi-yearly visits, I would stay with them for a couple of weeks. In the early morning, I would hear my dad get up and put on the coffee. I had once offered to get him a coffee maker that he could program so that the coffee would be ready for him when he rose at dawn. "No need," he said. "Coffee makes up pretty quick." Not picky, he would simply pour the first cup that came out and then reset the carafe so it could catch the rest. His chair faced the sliding glass doors that led out to the back deck, and he would sit and study the landscape before grabbing his lunch and thermos and heading out to cut some neighbor's hay.

It had been two years since my mother had died, and Dad had protected himself from that grief by plunging right back into work. The ranchers in the area knew that he could be trusted to do a good job and that age hadn't diminished his ability to handle a piece of machinery.

That summer, however, he and I traveled a bit. There were places I wanted to go and people I wanted to see.

CORNBREAD AND MILK

Most of us have most likely never experienced real Southern cornbread. Made with locally ground corn, freshly rendered hog lard, and baked in a cast iron skillet, old-fashioned Southern cornbread makes today's versions pale by comparison. Here's how to make real Southern cornbread:

Rub lard onto a black, well-seasoned cast iron skillet. Use real hog lard. If you just can't do that then use shortening, but it won't be authentic cornbread. Using a large serving spoon, dip a spoonful of lard and put it into the skillet. Preheat the oven to 425 degrees and put the skillet into the oven.

While the skillet is getting hot, assemble the rest of the ingredients. In a medium bowl, pour 3/4 cup of fresh buttermilk and one egg. Mix thoroughly with a fork—not an eggbeater. Add about 3/4 cup of freshly ground yellow cornmeal, 1/2 cup freshly ground flour, 1 tablespoon of baking powder, 1/2 teaspoon baking soda, and 1/2 teaspoon of salt. NO SUGAR! Mix until all ingredients are moistened; the batter will be lumpy. By this time your lard should be pretty hot. It should sizzle but not be burnt.

Pour the lard into the cornbread mixture. Mix the hot lard into the cornbread batter just enough to blend it, and then pour the batter into the skillet. Bake for about 20 minutes. The edges will be dark brown and the top a golden brown. Remove from the oven and immediately turn upside down onto a plate. Crumble into a bowl and serve hot with cold milk.

WE ARRIVED HOME at dinnertime, and Dad had a pot of beef stew in his crock-pot ready for us. After dinner, he went into the next room and turned on the TV while I cleaned up. Later I joined him.

"What did you eat Dad, when you were growing up?" I asked him.

He leaned back in his lounge chair, crossed his hands over his stomach, gazed off into the distance and spoke slowly and with assurance.

Every night our meal would be hot cornbread and cold sweet milk. Mom would make cornbread you could squeeze into a ball it was so moist. The milk was kept in a cistern—a stream that had been blocked up—and perishables would be put there. We poured out the sweet milk and would crumble that hot corn bread into that and eat it.

"Did you warm up the milk?" I asked.

No we didn't warm the milk—it was best cold.

"Did you have meat?"

Fresh meat might be a rabbit or a squirrel. Usually when you butchered you canned, cooked, cured—there was no way of keeping fresh meat. Dad raised a beef—we cooked it and canned it in jars. We'd make sausage and cook it and put it in fruit jars and pour rendered out grease (lard) and seal it and that would keep it—wouldn't spoil. When we needed it, we'd warm it up in a pan.

Shelby, my brother, and I used to crawdad fish—always lived on a crick, catchin' the crawdads, cookin' the tails, eat'n 'em.

We'd get a willow pole and tie a string to it and prob'ly we'd put a piece of side meat or bacon on the string and lower it into the hole. The crawdads would clamp on to that string, and we'd fish 'em out. Then we'd light a fire and cook them crawdads and eat 'em right there. They was kinda like lobster. We'd roast the tails and use them as bait to fish for catfish.

We had fish too. Sometimes we'd take a burlap bag and fill it with green walnuts. We'd pound that bag against a rock until it was a pulp, and then we'd lower it down into the stream. The water would turn black, and the walnuts would suck the oxygen right out, and the fish would come to the surface looking for air and Shelby an' I would grab 'em with our bare hands. I don't remember Mom cooking crawdads, but Shelby and I sure enjoyed 'em.

"Were there lots of walnut trees where you lived, Dad?"

31

You bet. That's how we got some of our meat. In spring, the woods was thick with black walnuts, persimmons, wild pecans, hickory nuts—hogs never had to be fed, they rooted. They were razorback hogs—you got to watch the buggers. We got chased up a tree once by a wild sow with tusks so long they would cut your legs off. Dad would catch 'em—he had a big ol' black and white dog, and he'd go down and put the dog on 'em and "ear" 'em down. He'd just bulldog the hogs just like a man pulled down a steer—that's how they'd catch 'em in the Fall.

People would get together to butcher. I've seen the time when the neighbors—usually two or three families—got together, and remember seeing seven or eight big old hogs hanging that they scraped. They didn't skin 'em. They'd slosh 'em in boiling water so that the hair would just slip off. They would hang all those old hogs up and the women had cast iron kettles and they'd skin off the meat and boil it and throw lye in it and make yellow soap. Then they would render the skins into lard, and that would preserve it all winter. Us kids, we would stand around and when they would boil a bunch of those rinds down, we eat those rinds—we'd have great big slabs of it—'cracklins' that's what they's called. That's where we got our soap and our lard—we didn't have no Crisco or anything—it was an all-day deal. To preserve the hogs, we'd use Morton's smoke to cure the hams and the bacon; we'd inject the marrow of the bones in those hams, and then rub that salt all over them an hang 'em to preserve 'em.

I can remember Mom taking that double-barrel shotgun, (JT still has that old shotgun) and the tree squirrels would come down, and the dog would come and tree the squirrels and she would shoot the squirrels. They're good eatin' so she got meat that way.

Note:

I find dad's fishing technique interesting. Later, I performed a quick Internet search that corroborates this method. It seems that toxins are released by the crushed hulls that act like carbon monoxide, replacing oxygen in the blood of the fish. It drives them to the surface without killing them where they are then easy prey. The method seems to have been used by many indigenous cultures. Dad had no idea how he learned it, but most likely it was an Indian technique that was observed and followed with success until it became just one of those "things that you just know."

We always had a good garden. The land was good bottomland. Dug the trees out by horse. We planted cotton and corn for sale and trade, and vegetables for the table. We had a hole in the ground with bushes over it for a root cellar, and during a tornado (a tornado is a straight wind, a cyclone is a funnel) it lifted Grandpa Freeman's barn up and hardly even damaged the barn. I don't remember seeing that happen, though.

I remember sleeping down there. You'd go below and a door would go over you. There was benches all around inside. It seems like we went in there a lot. We stored all canned goods, and lots of winter garden—carrots, onions, potatoes—under beds of straw. I remember the dark coolness and the smell of earth and vegetable all mixed together.

There was always lots of sweet milk. When I was 10, my dad had some cows down at a neighbor's field. Every morning before school, I would ride my bike over there and milk the cows. I would come back home with three milk cans, one for us, and one each for Mom's brothers and their wives. Then I would hop back on my bicycle and go to school.

"Well, you can't say you didn't earn your food! I'll bet you had some other work to do," I said.

That's right. We picked cotton and helped by dragging the sacks. We'd help out harvesting corn. They would put the kids on the down row, drive a wagon down the field and knock it over. The adults would pick the standing corn and us kids would grab the stalks that fell over and pick the ears off—there was no machinery to do anything like that at that time.

"What did you do for fun? There must have been some time for fun," I said, probing for more memories.

Yep, we worked hard but there was always time for fun. When it got cold, things would freeze up and get icy. I remember skating and sliding down from the house to the outhouse. We'd take a run and just slide all the way right up through the door. I guess it was probably about 100 yards away."

WHEN THE SAINTS GO MARCHING IN

The Ross Family Band: Ralph Ernest Ross – 4th from right

We all sang. We never had a pianist. Mom never did play the piano. But Dad's family had a brass band. He played the trumpet. They had a saxophone. Those people back in those years, they'd get together and have songfests—that's the only entertainment they had.

Jerry Ross

I was delighted to find this old photo of the family band and more evidence of my musical inheritance. No piano player? No wonder my Dad has always been at ease singing a cappella, launching into any tune comfortably with perfect intonation. I remember that Grandma Ross had a clear, strong, singing voice. No doubt, hymns made up a large part of the repertoire.

Dad believes there were no instruments at the brush arbor church he remembers but I have no doubt that the congregation sang with conviction, loudly and in harmony. How I wish I could have been a fly on the wall at the local songfests where people shared folksongs and hymns that had been handed down through generations as a means of community and fellowship. But then, my own youth was a little like that, come to think of it!

"Do you remember one particularly fun time?" I asked him.

The highlight of our life was to go to town with the cotton; we'd usually get a treat. Dad would buy us those wafers with cream in the middle—they were different colors. First one of those I ever had and man, we 'bout got sick of eat'n 'em. I remember going into town with Dad with a wagon load of cotton; they'd build sides about eight feet tall on them wagons and then we'd throw the sack up, then jump up and down and stomp on it 'cause cotton's light. We'd go to town and they had suction that uploaded it at the cotton gins; they had a pipe overhead and they'd move that pipe around and suck the cotton up in the gins, and then we'd come home after dark. They'd run it through the cotton gin and take the seeds out of it and clean it and put it in a cotton bale before they sent it to the textile places. A bale of cotton had burlap all around it and it had steel band and weighed about 1500 pounds.

The other highlight was taking a load of sorghum cane to the sorghum mill. That was something. We'd take a load of sorghum, which everybody raised, to the central sorghum mill and then unload it and they'd put it under rollers to suck the juice out of it, and that juice would go through a cooker and they'd boil it and boil it and the more they distilled it, the clearer it got, not like what you get in the stores, that black stuff—until it was about as clear as water and real light. Then they'd put it in troughs and stir it to cool it before they put it in jugs. It had a two-inch foam on it. And we boys, we'd find a board or a stick and use it like a paddle and we'd stand on those troughs and skim some of that froth off and eat it like it was like candy 'til we got sick. He chuckled at the memory.

"Now, did you sell this stuff for cash? How did that work?" I asked.

It was all a trade deal—barter—they'd squish it and distil it and bottle it for a share; it was the same way with the corn, same way with the wheat for flour. Never had to buy any wheat for flour, or molasses because it was a barter system. All Mom and Dad had to buy was pepper and salt and such 'cause they had their own meat and canned vegetables. We had to buy clothing of course. The cotton they would sell outright. The cotton gin would buy it and send it to the textile mill. The rest of the corn was cash too, except what was made into meal— kept that for ourselves.

"I remember Grandma but not Grandpa." I said. "He died when I was just a baby. What kind of parents were they?"

He was a real friendly, jovial person, Dad was—everyone liked Dad— 5' 9" and a solid husky man. Weighed 200 or 210. Never seen him mad but one time when he had a dog, that big border collie that he used to catch those hogs that were wild in the bottoms when he wanted some meat or a hog to sell. The dog would grab 'em by the ears. A man wanted the dog and tried to feed him and get him to stay, but the dog wouldn't stay so the man poisoned the dog. Dad found out about it and met him at the general store and accused him and the man wouldn't deny it and Dad knocked him clear into the street. Only time I ever saw Dad mad. Mom was fairly strict; she didn't say a lot but when she said something, we knew we had to do it. She made sure we had everything.

No, you didn't know him. Dad was only 55 years old when he died. He and your grandma were running the dairy out on Alta Mesa Road and one day your uncle JT just decided he would drop by for lunch. In the middle of a forkful, Dad just choked and fell over, dead. Now at that time, they didn't have a telephone and Mom didn't drive. It was providence that led JT to be there that day.

"I always remember Grandpa in that picture you have of him in the overalls sitting on the couch. Did you all wear overalls, Dad?"

I never saw a pair of waist pants 'til I come to California. On Sunday morning, we had our best pair of overalls, new and clean, we'd dress in them for church. My dad never got out of 'em—it was the work uniform. And Mom's dress almost dragged the floor.

DAD LOOKED TIRED to me, so we watched a little bull riding on the television, sitting as we always do, in companionable silence—that was until there was something about the bull riding or bull riders that he wanted to point out. But that is another story.

And so, that is how my dad saw his memories. They were poor, but he did not seem to remember that. My dad's sister Drothey laughed as she recalled a comment that my dad's cousin Don is known to have made.

"Why, we weren't poor! I remember that we had banana pudding every Sunday!"

How much did my Grandma and Grandpa hide from their children? Perhaps nothing. What we might consider poverty and deprivation today was just simply the way it was. At some point though, making a good living in Arkansas became a little too hard, so with emotional strength, hard work, and belief in God, they turned their backs on all they had known and headed out with optimism to a new place—a land of milk and honey—a place of opportunity where the sky was the limit. Instead of working for others, you could make it on your own.

THE WORKING MAN'S UNIFORM

Wrangler Company has been credited with developing the first denim overall sometime during the 20th century but their origin could be as early as 1750. However, it was during the Great Depression that these became the uniform for the working class. The deep and numerous pockets allowed for holding all sorts of tools, while the roomy fit allowed for freedom of movement. They seem to have represented America's fighting spirit as the country rebuilt itself after WWI. According to a book called *Vintage Denim* by David Little, "As the country recovered from the Depression, work clothes became something more; they fathered a style and a desire to belong to that working class."

**Ralph Ernest Ross and Jerry Ross
with Ernie, Karen, and Charlie Ross**

It's Cold Outside

The Old Made New

**Jerry Ross at 83, mowing the "backyard,"
viewed from the deck on his house in Bonanza.**

I HADN'T FORGOTTEN my vow to write a song every day, and the thought was there in the back of my mind as I woke up the next day. As the sun came up on my first day in Oregon, I looked out of my dad's sliding-glass door and saw the aspens make a feathery frame from above while the dry meadow provided a sharp contrast to the green pines of the distant mountains. I could see why he loved the place. It was peaceful with only chirping of the birds and the lowing of a cow or two to disturb the silence.

The High Desert is a place of contrasts. Cold winters and early frosts are countered by hot, dry summers. The terrain is open, with broad expanses of flat land fringed by mountains in the distance and populated by sagebrush and juniper. During the summer, the days can be very hot, but the nights almost always cool down. The temperatures can vary from 90 to 50 in a matter of hours.

I had been expecting the cool morning, but as I walked outside I actually felt colder than I was expecting to.

"Wow," I realized. "It's cold outside." That set up the song for day one. I found it interesting that the first inspiration came so easily.

The King James Bible states, "What has been will be again, what has been done will be done again; there is nothing new under the Sun." ~ Ecclesiastes 1:9. So, what do we creative types do with this message? Certainly the author of this biblical text did not envision computer chips and automobiles, but he did know of communication techniques and methods of conveyance. So, are computer chips and automobiles therefore not creative but rather a rehash of what had been?

Sometimes inspiration comes from something we already know but can make new through the unique vision that we all have. Song one shares a title and a partial premise with a classic American tune. "Baby, It's Cold Outside" is a pop standard with words and music by Frank Loesser. The lyrics in this duet are designed to be heard as a conversation between two people, marked as "mouse" and "wolf" on the printed score. Every line in the song features a statement from the "mouse" followed by a response from the "wolf".

From the Frank Loesser song, I borrowed a couple of things: the title and the premise. I used the "hook" from that song in my song, and I used the premise. When stripped down to a simplistic form, the premise is excuses. In the original song, the man tries to use the cold weather as an excuse to keep his lady friend from departing. In my song, the weather is used as an excuse for not visiting an old friend in order to apologize for a misunderstanding. After that, I guess, the similarity stops. If my song is a duet, then it is a duet of conscience. The inner voice urges the protagonist to do the right thing, while his conscience balks.

Words and melody always seem to come to me simultaneously, with lyrics often leading the melody. The underlying chord progressions are usually done afterwards; this sort of songwriting technique makes writing songs without an instrument possible for me.

Dad's house needed a cleaning as usual, so on this first day I gathered mop, broom, and rags, and commenced to the task while humming. As I sprinkled Ajax on the greasy buildup in the bathroom sink, I found myself humming the line to the hook of the song, "it's cold outside." I imagined two friends walking together. I needed a place for this—Second Street fit the rhythm.

Later, while dusting my mom's bedroom, I came across an old coat that hadn't been given away. I shrugged myself into it, remembering how she always made sure that we had new coats while saving the old ones for herself, holey pockets and all. "Maybe I'll put on my overcoat," I sang to myself. This became the first line of the song.

I reached for the broom and the mop and went to the kitchen. In the middle of the small room is wine rack. I remember buying that for her. It was exactly the right height to use as a small island, and it made a good resting place for her as she'd cook dinner, slowly making her way from the sink to the stove. In the corner of the connecting sitting room was a cast-iron stove that Dad loaded up every morning. Faced with these images, I sang as I scrub, "So I guess I'll just sit here by the fire and pour another glass of wine." And so it went. Swish, sing, scrub, sing, polish, sing.

On the following day, I made a trip into Klamath Falls to buy a recording device. I wouldn't always have the time to transcribe my Dad's tales, and I knew also that in order to continue with this songwriting experiment, I would have to have something to sing these songs into to jog my memory. While I might be able to write songs on the fly, I certainly cannot remember melodies without a great deal of repetition. One would certainly be crowded out by another and lost to me. So ended day one and song one.

It's Cold Outside

Maybe I'll put on my overcoat
and walk down to Second Street.
There's a friend I haven't seen in awhile,
and perhaps it's time we meet.
We've both forgotten what we argued about
and we're just too proud to admit it.
Maybe I'll knock on his door and smile.
But it's cold outside.
So I guess I'll just sit here by my fire
and pour another glass of wine
and watch the flames go higher and higher
and put it out of my mind.
I'll just put it right out of my mind.
Maybe it's time to return that scarf
he lent me so long ago.
It's not too far to that side of town;
I've been there so I know.
I remember how we used to walk that way
together to pass the time.
Now it would just bring me down
'cause it's oh, so cold outside.
Why should I be the one to make the first move?
He's as much to blame isn't he?
He knows where I live and he's got a coat –
why doesn't he walk over to me?
Maybe it's time to end this thing;
forget, that's the only way.
I guess I'll go see him right now –
or perhaps some other day.
You see, it's oh, so cold. It's cold outside—
it's cold outside.

THE SONG OF RUTH

Wherever you go, there shall I go.

Wherever you live, there shall I live.

Your people will be my people

And your God will be my God.

Ruth 1:16-17

King James Bible

Jerry and Helen Ross

I was livin' at home until I got married. Everyday I gave my money to my mom. Turns out she was savin' some for me and I had about $300 when I was married. Now, we wanted to go to Yosemite for our honeymoon. I had this portable welder that I'd been runnin' 'round the country doin' welding jobs for ranchers with. I sold it so that we could go to Yosemite.

Jerry Ross

Love and Marriage

MOM'S BEDROOM HAD BEEN unused since her death. She and Dad had taken to sleeping in separate rooms when her Parkinson's disease became advanced. His room was just next door where he could hear her wake in the night and comfort her against those intruders that visited her sometimes—hallucinations brought on by the medication—where he could hold and calm her when the shaking came, and she would not be calmed in any other way.

It possessed a large bed and its own bathroom, but I was more comfortable in the spare room on the twin bed which I shared with Dad's desk and the computer I had bought them. (I still smile with wonder at how my dad had taken to that machine, typing poorly spelled emails with two fingers and looking up recipes while checking the televised bull riding schedule.)

Even as she lay dying, and wanting to be there with her, I still could not lie down there with her but rather brought in a chair and placed it near her bed. Even in her coma, I knew that she knew I was there. On coming home after her death, I still did not wish to use this bed. Snug in the smaller bed in the spare room, perhaps I could conjure up the feeling that I was a child with two parents and that Mom was just sleeping and soon would make an appearance. She would come down the hallway, patiently, each hand fixed purposefully on her walker. A big smile would break on her face when she saw me, and she would begin the arduous task of living.

On the morning of day two, I awoke to the muffled sounds of the bulls in the field. The sun was still low on the horizon, and the cold High Desert air had replaced the heat of the previous afternoon. Through the door, I heard the dripping of water and the smell of coffee that signaled the beginning of each of my dad's days.

During that second year after Mom's death, my relationship with my dad continued to grow and deepen and I found myself grateful for that time. He was sitting in a straight-backed dining chair and facing the view of the distance hills framed by the sliding door. In another life there would have been a cigarette in his hand, but it has been a good 20 years since he quit smoking. "I'd be dead now if I hadn't quit," he said frequently.

"Well, hello!" he said heartily. Did you sleep good? There's coffee." I realized that the color was darker than usual and figured that he had put in an extra scoop just for me, having heard and acknowledged my mild observation that he drank his coffee weak. Perhaps he knew that I might use any excuse to take his big, old Pontiac the 15 minutes down the road to Bonanza where a very nice lady has a convenient espresso kiosk across from the high school.

For a while we sat in silence, both breathing in the desert's cool morning air. As the morning progressed, he began to chat about the happenings on nearby ranches and the activities of those who went to his church, particularly the Northcutt family who were close friends.

"Yep, them Northcutts, they're good people. I don't know what that church would do without them and that whole passel of little kids. They kind of think of me like a Grandpa—they don't have any of their own living. Last Sunday, I took a beef stew to the potluck after church— made it up in the crock-pot—and everyone just thought it was the best. Ate it all up. When I'm settin' to go home, Shelly handed me that crock pot all cleaned and refilled with a bunch of leftover." He laughed. "Yep, they take care of me."

At 83, my Dad was still a handsome man. I've seen pictures of him at 21 — chiseled, well-proportioned features, his long 6' 1" frame lean and muscular, light brown hair cut short in back and parted on the side, slicked back with a little more wave than William Holden but a little less than Alan Ladd, killer blue eyes and a cleft chin, a smile ready and wide, with just a little gum showing above even teeth.

My aunt has told me that he swept my mother off her feet. They were each 21. I coaxed my Dad into telling me about their early life.

AFTER WE WAS MARRIED, we moved up onto Woods Road. Man out there had a chicken ranch he owned, and his son owned that general store at Wilton. So we lived there first before we went to Jackson and did some mining for a year.

We were both 21. Tried to get into the army, but I had a heart murmur and a bad knee that I hurt playing football.

The year your mom and I spent at Jackson mining, the first year we were married—that was a really nice memorable year. The Wykes talked us into doing it. They were friends of the Hobday family. I worked awful hard up there and we just enjoyed being together. We thought we were going to make money but we never did. The year we spent mining was from '47 to '48. We had an old cabin there, just one room, no electricity, no running water. It didn't bother us. We were young. We had a lot of visitors, people coming up to see us.

Helen loved it up there. We brought her horse Sandy up there and she rode her some. It was nice hills and a stream and she could get out and walk those hills. First thing in the morning, we'd get up and light a fire—didn't have nothing but wood to burn and no running water; sometimes we would have to go get a bucket of water for breakfast, or go to the outhouses. Helen would go get groceries and cook on the woodstove—cookin' on wood is hard. But she didn't mind. She didn't have electricity at her home until just the year we got married. They were the last in California to get electricity down at Arno Road, so she wasn't used to running water or electricity. The Hobdays had a gas refrigerator and a gas cooking stove, but no lights. Mining was fun but it was about the hardest work I ever done in my life. We didn't have much machinery. It was all done by pick and shovel. There was this big pile of tailings that had been dug out of the mineshaft. The early miners had taken all the free gold out of them but there was a lot of piles that had gold. The biggest, longest tunnel anywhere went straight into a mountain, but it was locked.

All of the tailings had come out of it. We'd shove the tailings through a trammel (a rotating cylinder with holes in it) that would concentrate it down to real fine sand, then we'd shove it into a concentrating table and let the fines fall through; the table agitated back and forth with water running over it. It was rippled and slanted and the heavy stuff would stay behind and the little stuff would go off the bottom. It worked out and actually was a good experience. We never did get the gold fever—ready to go and get back down to civilization.

We worked a whole year and come up with, I think it was five barrels. Fifty-gallon barrels, two-thirds full each, and they weighed five tons, so there was a lot of gold in it to be that heavy. It had to be smelted at Selby, the only smelter left (by San Francisco) in the country, to get the gold out. So we loaded it into Dad's old two-and-a-half ton, that same old '29 Chevy we come out to California in, and we took it into Selby to be smelted. Out of the five ton of ore we took down there, our share was only $128 for the whole year. In the process of smelting it, they run it through rollers to crush it real fine. A lot of that free gold sticks to those rollers, and they never say nothing about that. They'd let it go on through and then they'd scrape the rollers and take our free gold. They stole all that gold from us. That was a year of experience. After that year we had no place to go, so we came back and moved our bed, table, and chairs into your grandma and grandpa's garage. The garage was not sealed, so we nailed rolls of embossed paper up and down those studs. There was no sink or bathroom; later we moved to the old Martin place on Woods Road.

Drothey and Alice Ross (cousin) at the Ross house in Alta Mesa.

He leaned back as if that was all he had to say on that subject. In the years that followed his marriage, Dad traded his white t-shirt for a khaki work shirt, which he rolled up to midway between his elbow and wrist. Sometime in his twenties, T-shirts became undershirts, and I never again saw him with short sleeves.

When work shirts were traded for cowboy duds, even then the sleeves stayed rolled up most of the time. But the charm stayed. He aged well, gaining weight only in his later years, his features staying chiseled, his laugh staying large, and those blue eyes and cleft chin still making an impression. It seems unusual that a man so handsome should be so totally uninterested in that handsomeness. Never the dandy, he appeared to not look at another woman after he married my mother and seemed totally oblivious to (or chose to ignore) glances that might be directed his way. He sported simple clothing styles and in the years I knew him seemed content with a couple of pairs of blue jeans and a few Western shirts—with a few short sleeved Hanes underneath. When I look at his face I see the good looks still peeking out, softened by the extra folds of age, and I feel tenderness. His eyes still have that sparkle and his laugh is as big as ever but he seems vulnerable. Such a mighty man he was. A man's man. A man who loved the company of men and men's pursuits. A gun, a horse, a dog, a pickup—such were his needs.

I know that he is not averse to knowing he is admired, however. The year after I wrote these songs, I returned to take him on another trip and we visited his old friend, Claude, who was residing in an adult-care facility in Stockton, California. As Dad, his friend Claude, and my uncle JT sat around the luncheon table and laughed, a woman who looked to be in her late 70's or early 80's approached the table.

"You're all having such a good time; I just had to come over." She glanced down at my Dad who was nearest to her and put her hand on his shoulder. "Are you Irish? You look Irish; my husband was Irish."

"Oh, I guess I'm some Irish but mostly Scots and English," Dad replied.

"Are you married?" she asked.

"He was," I interrupted.

"That'll do," she said.

Claude's daughter, Sally, decided that it must be the cowboy hat my

Dad was wearing that was the major attraction. She said to her dad, "We should go get your cowboy hat."

The lady's eyes flickered around the table and took in Claude and JT.

"No, I like this one," she said, patting my Dad on the shoulder.

Dad told this story for weeks afterwards, laughing his big laugh. "Not a bad looking' woman, either," he'd say.

You've still got it, Jerry. The years have taken a toll on his body. Bad knees, torn apart from long ago football injuries, cause him to shuffle in his cowboy boots. I remember the accidents he's had: a runaway harvester that decided to run over him and hours spent beneath a fallen mare while suffering from a few broken ribs. Old back injuries bend him over at his full belly. I sometimes see him, after a bit of exertion, leaning against a car or table just catching his breath a little. But when he tells a story and his blue eyes crinkle and his mouth turns up with just the hint of a smile, I can still see him at 21— the heartthrob that swept my mother off her feet.

In a canyon, in a cavern, excavating for a mine,
dwelt a miner, 49'er and his daughter, Clementine.

WHO HASN'T HEARD of the great California gold rush? Thousands came from all over the world to stake their claims—from everywhere they traveled months to arrive by steamer to the Pacific shores and by foot across the United States, facing the harsh realities of disease and starvation. It changed the state forever and embedded in our minds images of the lone prospector, his donkey tethered nearby, hunched over a burbling brook gold pan in hand, his slouch hat dirty and weathered. He searched for the easy gold, but he sometimes had to dig with his pick and shovel to dislodge what was just below the surface. It was

"pay dirt" time when he happened on a particularly lucrative pile.

However it was not the prospector that truly changed the California landscape but rather the large mining companies that, with their hydraulic jets, learned to dislodge large chunks of rock from hillsides directing it into sluices that separated the rock from the gold, or pulverized the rock into small particles via dynamite and chemicals. This latter method produced the "tailings" that my dad mentioned. They were also known as slime, leach residues, tails, and slickens.

From the large mine tunnel of the Amador Queen, one of the mines in the lucrative gold belt of the Jackson-Plymouth area, came the tailings that drew my mom and dad and other modern day prospectors. Piled in mounds around the closed mine shaft, gold was still there. It was not easy gold and was polluted by the mercury and arsenic used to extract it in the first place. One hundred years after gold fever swept the state, people continued to gravitate towards these mounds, seeking their fortune.

There is still plenty of gold in California, though harder to get to and controlled by heavy environmental regulations. But the romance is still there, floating to the top of the sludge of reality: two young newlyweds living on love and dreams in a small cabin in the pines of California in 1947.

Blue Dress
Song From An Image

Time it was,
And what a time it was
It was . . .
A time of innocence
A time of confidences
Long ago . . . it must be . . .
I have a photograph
Preserve your memories
They're all that's left you.
                    Paul Simon, *"Bookends"*

IT WAS INTERESTING that on day two my songwriting should have its impetus in another song. I had brought something with me on that second year anniversary of my mother's death. I had written a song called "Like an Angel," recorded it, and made a few CDs to give to family and friends.

My mother was a gifted singer. Her voice was mellow and sweet, the kind that was often called upon to sing at the locals events such as weddings and funerals. She didn't think much about this gift, she only knew that she loved to sing, especially hymns. She thought so little on it, that it never occurred to her to have her voice recorded, and I guess it didn't occur to anyone else much to my sorrow. In my song, I made a point to remind the world that "she sang like an angel, sang like they do."

For that CD cover, I had chosen a picture that I had come across in my mother's things when I was cleaning after her death.

"I don't remember ever seeing this picture Dad. When was it taken," I asked him.

"Well, we were engaged to be married in June and I remember that your mom bought that dress at Christmas. I didn't know that she intended to have a picture taken in it to give me as a Christmas present.

One day she asked me to take her to town so I did. She just said that she had some errands to do. It turns out she wanted to pick up the photos but wanted to keep it a surprise from me; but the photographer was busy, so it took a lot longer to get the photos than she expected, and when she got back to the car where I was waiting she felt she needed to apologize for taking so long, so she blurted out that she had been getting the photos. When she realized that she had let the secret out, she blushed."

At this point my Dad started to laugh.

"That was just like your Mom; always worried about getting in the way or upsetting anyone." His eyes started to tear up and the tone of the laughter changed as he choked back the emotion.

That was the impetus for this next song. I took some liberties with the story in the song, however, not intentionally. I just hadn't fully caught all of the details. When I realized that I had altered the story slightly, I didn't change it. Songwriting is not always about accuracy but rather about conveying mood and message.

53

That day was also spent at Dad's house as we prepared to head out traveling the next day. I took a trip into Klamath Falls to do some errands for him (and to pick up that recording device) and while I drove I thought about that picture. Mom is lovely in the photo. Only my brother Ernie inherited her dark hair and eyes—the rest of us are fair like Dad. So the eyes began to stand out for me as I saw them in contrast to that white collar and hum "it brought out the darkness of her eyes."

It wasn't a stretch to come up with the rest of the chorus: young, sweet, eager, forgetting the surprise. It made a great refrain. The rest of the song was just imagination as I tried to visualize this story. Checking her lipstick in the drugstore mirror just seems like something she would have done and puts the song into the time period. Whether my dad would have read a paper, I doubt, but it fits the meter and is another visual for the listener to visualize.

As I parked the Pontiac and got out at Albertson's grocery store, I imagined her coming out, opening the door, and getting back in beside him. "Sidles" is an old-fashioned word but very expressive in its meaning. Then, I see those eyes again—dancing, irrepressible, delighted with her own creativity.

The rest came from my Dad's story and just relates the truth.

I remember traveling around with Dad after she died. I was touched by how docile he was as he, for once, made no argument as I did the driving. I remember having felt the need to shield him from the sight as the ambulance attendants came into the house to carry his lifelong companion out the door on a stretcher.

"Come out on the porch, Dad," I said. "You don't need to see this." He went willingly. Later, as we accomplished those tasks that needed to be done, as we drove back and forth from the funeral and then out to the graveyard, he spoke often of her beauty, her creativity, and her hard work.

Your mom was real beautiful. And she was so talented. Never was an instrument she couldn't play.

At the end of her life she began painting again, and Dad made sure that very special friends and family received paintings of hers after she died. He was so proud to give them away. As he choked back the tears and related her sweet, simple mistake, my eyes flit over to the lift chair that I had bought her when it was clear that getting out of the chair was difficult. I remember my Dad commenting once, "Sometimes when I'm watching TV, and something funny happens, I look over to see if Mom saw and I expect her to be there."

"An empty chair, a presence gone, all that's left's a photograph
—a gift for her lover through the years."

"Blue Dress" is a story song—a song based on a personal narrative. It also is response to the picture itself. The photograph says just a few things about my mother but when coupled with the story my dad related, it becomes much more. Certainly, it was my mother who shaped my earlier musical years, who made sure that I got to the library to take out my two dozen books every couple of weeks. Not an avid reader herself, she seemed to understand that need in me with a mother's intuitiveness.

She taught me to how to read music and play the piano, and I remember her collection of sheet music: Sons of the Pioneers, Roy Rogers and Dale Evans, and Gene Autry.

Everyone thinks of my Dad as the cowboy, but my mom was a horse-woman before my Dad, and her bedroom was covered with pictures of horses and the old West. In her drawing and painting, horses were a consistent theme.

When Eric Kilburn, who recorded several tracks for my "Gemini Rising" CD at his Wellspring Studio in Acton, Massachusetts, heard this song he said, "It's like an old Carter Family song."

I guess that was what felt right with this song. It is an old-fashioned song, written about an old-fashioned girl. The story was my inspiration, and bringing it to song meant digging into my past and into the feeling that my mother's youth evoked in me.

Lyrics and melody—what shapes what? In my case, I write them simultaneously. The melody seems to evolve in tandem with the words, as happened in this case. Everything combined to give this song an "old-timey" feel and it pretty much wrote itself.

Blue Dress

She wore a blue dress with a white collar.
It brought out the darkness of her eyes.
Young and sweet and eager trying hard to please,
she forgot it was to be a surprise.
Soon to be married they went driving into town.
She said there is an errand I must run.
He said sure no problem, I'll just sit and read the paper
and I'll be waiting for you when you're done.
She caught her reflection in the drugstore window,
paused a moment, checked her lipstick for smears
then posed for the camera, lips parted, smiling shyly,
a gift for her lover through the years.
She opened up the car door,
sidled over, squeezed his arm,
her deed still dancing in her eyes.
Then without thinking, she just blurted out her story,
she forgot it was to be a surprise.
When champagne's uncorked
those bubbles just start rising.
How could she suppress a thing so grand?
She blushed when she remembered
it was meant to be a secret
until she had that photo in her hand.
Sixty years later he recalls it all with laughter,
trying hard to blink back the tears.
An empty chair, a presence gone,
all that's left's a photograph,
A gift for her lover through the years.
She wore a blue dress with a white collar.
It brought out the darkness of her eyes.

THE ARKANSAS TRAVELER

This term in the 20th century is the name of a fiddle tune, a riverboat, a newspaper, and a baseball team and is used in general to describe anyone from Arkansas. Specifically, the term goes back to a folk tale, circa 1840. In the tale, a stranger arrives at the door of an Arkansas cabin. He is tired and hungry and looking for a place to stop for the night. He finds the inhabitant of the cabin playing a fiddle tune that he doesn't seem to be able to finish.

The owner of the cabin is not the least hospitable and ignores the stranger while continuing to play this unfinished tune. Finally frustrated, the traveler grabs the fiddle and finishes the tune. This transforms the cabin owner into the most hospitable of hosts and he invites the stranger in. In many versions of this story, the cabin owner is painted as an ignorant hillbilly and made the brunt of a humorous anecdote, perpetuating the negative connotations of the rural Arkansas resident.

A fiddle tune called "The Arkansas Traveler" has been credited to many people and began to circulate with that title, and a famous picture painted by Edward Payson Washbourne in 1856 seemed to corroborate the "outsider" versus hillbilly image that was a popular stereotype.

Some people felt that this story was disastrous to Arkansas' image, but ultimately it simply reinforces the high esteem in which the mountain folk held music.

THE MIGRANT ROAD

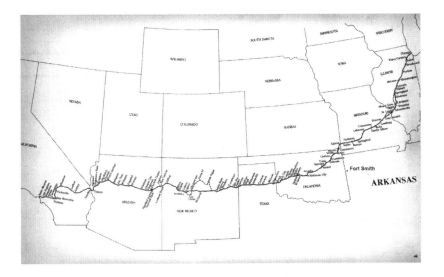

Highway 66 is the main migrant road. 66—the long concrete path across the country, waving gently up and down the map, from Mississippi to Bakersfield—over the red lands and the gray lands, twisting up into the mountains, crossing the Divide, and down into bright and terrible desert, and across the desert to the mountains again, and into the rich California valleys.

66 is the path of a people in flight, refugees from dust and shrinking land, from the thunder of the tractors and shrinking ownership, from the desert's slow northward invasion, from the twisting winds that howl up out of Texas, from the floods that bring no richness to the land and steal what richness is there. From all of these the people are in flight, and they come into 66 from the tributary side roads, from the wagon trucks and the rutted country roads. 66 is the mother road, the road of flight.

John Steinbeck, *The Grapes of Wrath*

Journey Past

THERE IS SOMETHING very special about the High Desert country. At first glance, it might seem to be the last place people would choose to settle. In New England, people settled near the streams and rivers, those rivulets of commerce that transported the fruits of their labors to other cities and far away countries, quenched the thirst of their sheep and cattle, and watered their crops.

The sparseness of water is noticeable in the High Desert landscape. As in other places, the larger towns are settled near whatever lake or river might happen to be there, but the settlers went further afield, making homes and ranches in the rocky, juniper dotted hills where wells go deep.

On day three, I woke as usual to the cool air ruffling the curtain beside my bed and was invigorated. I always slept well there—the cool nights, the deep silence, and the absence of light create a little cocoon that seemed to suit the curve of my body.

Dad was, as always, sitting facing the glass doors holding his premature cup of coffee, as the rest of the water gurgled and sputtered into the carafe at his side. "Well, good morning, Jane." My dad's voice, still as Arkansas as ever, was always hearty and lifted with a slight inflection at the end of the sentence. "Did you sleep good"?

"I slept good. What time did you want to get going?"

I waited until most of the water had dripped through and poured myself a cup. A glance at Mr. Coffee told me that he was due for a good cleaning, as was the small marble slab that he rested upon. I had bought Dad the slab last summer; he tended to leave the coffee on all morning and the heat took its toll on the Formica that covered the peninsula.

"Oh, I suspect 'bout 10 or 11 is ok. That'd put us into Daryl's when he's getting off work. He's usually home by four."

"No fires?" My brother worked for the BLM (Bureau of Land Management) and when he wasn't dealing with the issues of water management he operated a forklift during fire season. The dry, open country can go up like a match in the summertime.

"Nope. Says he should be ok. They're having a party for Chelsea before she goes back to school so we'll be seeing a lot of Peilas."

Chelsea, my niece, was attending Eastern Washington University, and the Peilas are my sister-in-law's family. Ann is one of 11 children and there would undoubtedly be a great number of them at the party.

"We could leave a little earlier and plan to stop for lunch in Lakeview," I suggested.

"Sure, we could do that."

The drive to Burns, Oregon, would take us about four hours. Lake - view, a town of about 2600 people, was about 90 minutes away and did indeed border a lake.

The drive over Bly Mountain could be treacherous in the winter but in July it was clear and dry and the high country was a nice change from the desert. Juniper gave way to spruce and pine, and traffic was sparse consisting mostly of cross-country truckers.

Whenever we traveled past the junction of US 97 and onto the Bly Mountain cut-off Dad always said the same thing. "Your mom looked at a house up here. I'm glad we didn't get a place way out here. I wouldn't have wanted to live a way out here."

Dad likes his space, and he would never be able to live in a city or even a small town. But I found it interesting that even he has his limits. Bly Mountain cut–off is a 'fur piece' from friends and church, and even though he doesn't want to be looking into anyone's windows, he appreciates good neighbors and like–minded ranchers being nearby.

My mind wandered back to Alicia, Arkansas. It must have been the same there. He might have been in the "middle of nowhere" but friends, family, and comradeship were always close by.

All of my dad's memories are filled with family and companionship.

Perhaps that is why they are always filled with optimism and fun.

His memories are different from the image I have of the displaced Southerner I had read about in John Steinbeck's novel, *The Grapes of Wrath*. The Oklahoma farmers had owned their own property until an extreme drought, the advent of mechanization, and increasing debt led to bank ownership and forced their removal. But unlike Steinbeck's Joad family who were forced from their land, the Rosses seem to have left voluntarily like many others who were just looking for a better life.

On that day's drive, I decided to find out a little bit about another trip he took 72 years ago.

**JT Ross, Emma Ross, and Dorothia (Drothey) Ross prepare
to leave Arkansas in their new, improvised home.**

*"The family met at the most important place, near the truck . . .
this was the new hearth, the living center of the family, half passenger
car and half truck— high sided and clumsy. . ."*

John Steinbeck, *The Grapes of Wrath*

ARKANSAS DURING THE DEPRESSION

The time I spent sitting cross-legged on the floor of the ASI leafing through books gave me some insight into how the Depression started in Arkansas and how it affected its inhabitants. It wasn't just one major catastrophe that brought the Depression to Arkansas. Things began to worsen after the great flood of 1927. It covered over four million acres and over one hundred people drowned. As the waters receded, the state began to recover but then came the crash. One hundred banks closed down. If that weren't bad enough, a long drought began—the temperatures soared to 100 degrees everyday. The Red Cross had to come in to help and they fed over 180,000 families.

The culmination of these events was to take what was already a very poor state and bury it deeper in the dust of poverty. Arkansas was a largely rural state, with over 80% of the residents living on farms or in villages. The major economic system centered around cotton and the culture of the tenant farmer. The system favored the landowner, and the tenant farmer was dependent on the plantation community. This was a form of what has been called "voluntary serfdom" and sharecroppers, as they were known, raised the crops and gave a large portion of that crop to the landowner who took the responsibility for weighing the crops and giving the tenant his credit in seed.

As the Depression deepened and squeezed the landlord, and as tractors and seasonal labor forced out the sharecropper, families saw their only recourse was to take to the road. [However, the Arkansas migration was not as huge as it was in other states and only 213,000 emigrated in the 30's, which was less than had emigrated in the 20's.]

In 1936, the hard times lingered. The small farmers could not afford to pay their laborers. So, Emma and Ralph Ross, along with their four children and a brother and his wife, like so many others piled into a small, modified truck and headed West.

JOURNEY TO A NEW LIFE

I could imagine that the Ross family left Arkansas with misgivings; they did leave behind family and friends that they knew they would never see again. They left behind many possessions that could not fit into the truck. I was sure that they left with the same fears and anticipations as anyone might but this emigration thing was not new; their fathers before them had done it and lived through it and prospered. They also took with them their religious faith, their work ethic, and hopefulness. Dad told me what he could remember of that journey long ago.

We didn't live in the dust bowl. I don't know exactly why Dad decided to leave at this particular time, but I'm sure it was because it was becoming harder to make a living. He needed to feed a family; maybe he hoped it would be easier to own something out there in California. We were always hearing about California, about how nice the weather was and how many jobs there were.

I was eleven, JT was five, Shelby was about thirteen and Drothey only six months.

Don't know how Dad got the money to buy the truck we came in. The first car I remember was an old Essex, kind of like a touring car. I imagine it was the first he ever bought, and he probably traded it for that old Chevy pickup that we drove to California— '29 ton-and-a-half truck, and he built a house on the top of it, twelve by seven, not a very big house for everyone. It had a bed that Mom and Drothey slept in at night. Not much furniture.

That's for sure. I don't remember what we used as furniture or stoves. We had everything we owned in the back of the truck. We only brought clothes and left the housekeeping stuff behind. We had nothing to entertain us—no books, nothing, not even cards; we had dominos. Actually in our era, cards was a sin, associated with gambling.

Mom didn't know how to drive, so Dad did it all. We would pull off to the side of road under the trees and stop at a store and pick up some bologna and light bread—it was a treat for us to get a loaf of bakery bread. Mom's was good, but this was a treat.

We went straight through to Arizona and stopped for the winter 'cause we ran out of gas. JT had some mastoid problem too, and we stopped 'til he got better. Dad made enough money in Phoenix to buy gas and feed us until we got to California, just outside of Los Angeles.

I can't really remember how long it took us to get to Phoenix, but I remember that we wintered there. Dad, Mom, Shelby and I would pick fruit while JT would watch Drothey. JT and Drothey came along to the fields; they weren't left alone to fend totally for themselves. But things were different in those days and kids grew up pretty quick.

"We hear a lot about those tent cities that existed during those days. Did you ever live in one?" I asked.

In Arizona we lived in a tent city. There would be a part of those tent cities out in the orange orchards. We had a lot of fun in Arizona— the first time we could pick oranges. In Arkansas, we might get an orange and a candy cane for Christmas. We liked those oranges but we couldn't afford to buy them, and in Phoenix you could just reach up and get one any time you wanted.

The doves wintered there and they were thick and we made a slingshot and my cousin Gib and I would go out and shoot them. B.F. Goodrich that Dad worked for raised cotton and sheep for the fibers for their tires and they had big pastures of burros that shepherds used to herd the sheep. Three or four of us kids would go out at night and we'd rope those donkeys and we'd gentle 'em down and ride 'em over the desert until we got caught—we were kind of in a little bit of trouble there for a while—at least we broke the donkeys for 'em to ride. We had a lot of fun doing that.

It was quite a camp that you lived in; they had tents with wood floors and cotton fabric over them. There were lots of people all in the same fix we were in, coming from Arkansas or Oklahoma at the end of the Depression and no one had any money at all. But Mom and Dad always managed to have clothes for our backs and food on the table. I was old enough to pick but had to go to school too, so on Saturday we would help Mom and Dad; they'd pay by the pound so whatever we picked we put in their hopper and it paid more. We didn't have a lot but we didn't need a lot.

"So you went to school Dad? How did you manage that?"

My school in Arkansas was one room. I went there regularly until we left. Then we went to school all across the country when we traveled from Arkansas. We went to the town schools as we went across the country. Buses would come to the tent cities and take us into town.

THE PROVINCE OF WOMEN

In the little houses
the tenant people sifted their belongings
and the belongings of their fathers
and of their grandfathers.
Picked over their possessions
for the journey to the West.
The men were ruthless
because the past had been spoiled,
but the women knew
how the past would
cry to them in the coming days.

John Steinbeck, *The Grapes of Wrath*

LATER I HAD the opportunity to talk to my dad's family, and I received some additional insights into these times. I asked my Aunt Janice if Grandma Ross had ever talked about those days. Janice is married to my dad's brother, JT. (Now JT are not initials for other names. My two great grandfathers were John Thomas and Joseph Elbin and that is where Grandma got the JT from, but on his birth certificate it is just JT.)

Aunt Janice has been like another mother to me. Her daughter, Terri, was my best friend growing up, and I spent a lot of time at their home in Florin, California, a house that my uncle had built. She is a sweet and lovely person, always pleasant and laughing. Her daughter inherited her tendency to look into your eyes while she talks, and nod, and say "uh huh, uh huh," conveying a genuine interest in what you have to say. So it might be natural that it was Aunt Janice who fed me a small anecdote that would never have come from my dad's lips.

Sitting at dinner in the house that JT converted from an office into a beautiful gem of a retirement home, Janice listened to the material I had collected, as always nodding and saying "uh huh, uh huh" in a way that made me know that she was really listening. Then, with her brown eyes expressive and her voice soft and tender she said, "Your grandma once told me that as the family prepared to leave Arkansas, her mother looked at her sadly and said, 'I will never see you again.'"

A short phrase but ripe with meaning. What about those that were left behind? In the same way that parents said goodbye to their children as they apprenticed them to strangers so that they might have a better life in some foreign land, in the same way that families were ripped apart and sent to prison camps during the Holocaust never to meet again, in the same way that immigrants throughout time have left what they know and love because they could no longer sustain a family or because their lives were in peril, my grandma and grandpa had hitched their converted truck to a star—a star called California—knowing that they might never see their aging parents again.

True to her prediction, my grandmother never saw her mother again, but her father lived long enough to make the trek out to California 15 years after his daughter left Arkansas.

**Emma Freeman Ross, Joseph Freeman, Jerry and great-grandkids
Karen, Ernie, and Charlie**

Drothey, my dad's youngest sister, was only six months old when she left Arkansas and so remembers nothing of that trip, but she does remember something that, again, my dad might not have noticed or not thought to tell me. She would have been only seven years old when Great Grandma Alice passed away but my Aunt Drothey remembers, even at that tender age, that my Grandpa cried when he got the news.

Drothey is another aunt that I consider a second mother. (It is Dorothia on her birth certiciate, but we've only known her as Drothey. In fact, I think that she didn't find out until recently that her "real" name was Dorothia. Her middle name is Jane, and I am named after her.)

She is 11 years younger than my dad, and it was always a fun treat to go to her house and stay over with my sister Karen and cousin, Terri. She is and always was, beautiful, with high cheekbones, a straight nose, and laughing eyes. She shares the Ross laugh that I remember my grandma having and know that my Dad has, and a wicked sense of humor. And Drothey, like Janice, would be most likely to put that human touch to memory.

Tears and love are not the exclusive province of women but for some reason, women seem to remember the emotional things. They remember the tears and the pain. Men are not exempt, of course, from the pain of leave-taking or the love of family, but it took two aunts to remember and to relate these small emotional moments.

Janice, Jane, and Drothey

CALIFORNIA – THE FIRST FIVE YEARS

1940: Shelby (Jerry's brother), Sam (a cousin), Jerry, Selby (a cousin)

All things considered, the rural migrants, especially from the southwestern states, made calculated decisions to go to California; they were not merely "blown out" or "tractored out"—rather, they had reduced their risks to tolerable, if not manageable, proportions. Those who were very poor generally did not go. Those who did would participate in a cotton farming economy with which they were familiar. Many were influenced by the reliable judgments of California residents whom they already knew. They brought their families with them to ensure their productivity. Their families of origin had made these kinds of moves before, and they, their heirs, were living proof of the foresight of those decisions. Furthermore, they brought with them confidence in their own rural-based cultural heritage—hard work, family cooperation, community with kindred folk, and prayer—that would work anywhere. The hopefulness of Okies going to California in the 1930s was something they brought with them.

(McGovern 112)

WE PULLED INTO LAKEVIEW and headed to Jerry's Restaurant for lunch.

"Do they give you a discount here, Dad, since the place is named after you?" I asked.

"No, they don't —dirty varmints. I'll have to see into that," he said in a semi-serious tone.

Dad turned down the offer of coffee. "Don't drink any coffee after the mornin'," he said. I smiled at another age-related change from a man for whom coffee was almost the only beverage in existence at one time.

As we waited for our meal, I asked him, "What did you do when you got to California Dad? Where did you live?"

First we went to those places that raised fruit and we lived in tent cities; there was lots of people looking for work, so they made these tent cities. There would be hundreds of people living in those tent cities.

Wasn't too long before we headed to Arroyo Grande. We didn't follow the fruit too long. I don't remember why we went to Arroyo Grande but maybe someone told Dad about the eucalyptus groves and the wood business. We still had that old '29 Chevy. I remember driving down "the Grapevine" coming into L.A. The truck's brakes started to fail, and me and Shelby jumped out and threw rocks and pebbles beneath the smoking wheels to slow it down and bring it to a halt.

We were in a tent in Arroyo Grande too, but we put it on rented land. When we got to the coast, there were eucalyptus groves. When Dad was cutting wood in the wood yard, he bought three cows and he rented a pasture in the orchard about six to seven miles away, and I'd ride over in the morning and bring milk home and go to school— I was 13 or 14—on my bike. Do it again in the afternoon.

Dad charged so much a cord and Filipinos were the ones who bought the wood. There was vegetable farms nearby and Filipinos worked 'em and then lived in a commune and they had a great big communal bathhouse and they bought most of the wood to fire their baths. We got $5 a cord for us.

Started in the fifth grade but I sent myself back to the fourth because I didn't think I was as smart as those California kids; it meant I didn't have to study and got good grades. It put me a year behind though.

It was fun when we got to California. We got to eat out of a store. We had family with us. Dad's brother Ardy was married to Mom's sister Gertie and they had followed us out West. My cousins Don and Gilbert were just like brothers, and we did everything together. Eventually we had other aunts, uncles and cousins out there too.

The ocean was especially fun. Yeah, there was a big bunch of sand hills between the mesa and the ocean, and we'd walk across those sand hills. It was white sand—no brush on it or nothin'. We'd spread out and scare the cottontails and pick 'em off with our slingshots. We'd always go swimming at Christmas so we could tell the folks back home, because it was snow and ice back there; actually that was the warmest time—the water was warmer around Christmas than in the summer. We had a lot of fun playing in those old sand hills. We would find a small eucalyptus tree and strip the bark off of it. Underneath it was smooth. Using three branches we put together a means of conveyance. Two branches formed the sides and the third connected the sides. Grabbing on to the centerpiece, we took turns sliding down the Mesa.

After lunch, we went back to the truck and left Lakeview heading towards Burns. We still had almost three hours of driving left— plenty of time to continue with the story.

"One day there was a Japanese Trader (a ship) out in the ocean carrying lumber. It ran aground and in order to get him off of the sandbar they had to throw all of the lumber off and throw it into the ocean and it started washing up on the beach and everyone in the country was draggin' it out—my dad and uncle and Shelby my older brother—I was too young—would go out there and drag that lumber and stack it; they come around and wanted it back but they did pay us a price for it.

Note:

I later got a chance to talk to Dad's younger brother, JT. He is six years younger than Dad and doesn't remember as much, but I asked him about that time on the California coast. JT is a soft-spoken man with a fine bass voice and a wry understated sense of humor; he has always been a favorite of mine, even though he tends to tease me mercilessly. JT reminisced a bit. It seems that he was a prime target for sibling mischief. "If I'd a had a gun, I'd a shot him." He laughed. "Your dad put me in an old tire and rolled me down a hill!" But he remembered a life of active fun in which he was a participant instead of the target. "I remember back in the eucalyptus groves we had games we'd play. Sometimes two of us would climb up a slender, willowy kind of tree and with our weight cause it to go lean backward; then, one of use would jump off which would then propel the other out at an arc into the air."

Over time, Dad's business expanded and he was selling cooking and firewood down in L.A. Yeah, if Mom's health hadn't been bad and we could have stayed over there, Dad probably would have been a rich man. But it was damp and foggy. She stayed sick all the time. When we left, Dad had enough to buy a 1940 Chevy.

By the time we left Arroyo Grande, we had a house to live in; the first year we had a walled up tent. We spent five years there. Uncle Ardy and Gertie, another of mom's sisters, Edith, and her husband, John. I remember that place real well. The year that JT, Janice, Drothey and Norman (Drothey's husband), your mom and I went back to visit was 50 years exactly from the time we'd left. I could go right to things—it had all changed—bits and pieces sold off but I found the place where the wood yard was and where we had our tent.

We headed upstate back towards Yuba City because there were jobs in Camp Beale, the Air Force base. Shelby and Dad and I worked in it, and Uncle Ardy–Gib was too young.

I made more money than Dad and Shelby because I got in with the boss on the bone yard where they would haul all of the used lumber and the forms that they made cement with; he decided he needed a helper and made me supervisor over about 25 men. They'd look at me a little, (I was only 16 years old) but did as I said. We gave all of our money to Mom and Dad as we made it. I never kept any for myself.

While in Yuba City, Dad bought an almond orchard and house but never lived in it; he traded it for a Guernsey dairy in Alta Mesa with 80 cows. He could make a living milking. He bought cows and equipment. Everything went into cans and not bulk tank trucks.

I LET THIS SETTLE IN A MINUTE, imagining a young Jerry in the brashness of youth, giving orders to men his senior and this does not seem a bit implausible, knowing what I know of his natural leadership qualities. I asked my aunt Drothey what she thought of it. "Oh, I don't doubt that at all," she said. "Your dad always had a way about him that made people look up and respect him."

"You know, Dad, in the books we always read of people being without work—at least during the Depression. Do you remember ever needing work?" I asked.

I don't remember ever being without work. It seems that Dad and Mom and Shelby always had some job or another. It didn't seem like hard times. We always had food and clothing and shelter. Everyone else was pretty much in the same boat, and it did not strike us that we had any more or less than everyone else we knew.

"Now, you were 16 when you moved to Alta Mesa right? Were you still in school? What did you guys do for fun in those days?"

I went to Elk Grove High School. I remember good times. For fun we rode horses, hunted rabbits and ducks. We would go out at night where they had planted oats for hay. I had my old Studebaker with a mother-in-law seat in back and guys would be standing on the back and all around the fenders and we go out in these fields to shoot jack rabbits, thicker than hair on a dog's back.

We'd get maybe 35 of 40 of those in a night and a few times run out of ammo and then we'd chase after them with car and spotlight until they stopped and then hold the spotlight on them and the rest of us would go way around and go off the side and hit 'em with sticks, (laughs). There were too many of them and they ate of the crops and spread disease, so no one minded. We also did a lot of frog giggin'.

We'd go out at night with a flashlight and shine the light on 'em and gig 'em. After I had a family, your sister Karen would go along with a gunnysack carrying those frogs for us and she'd get bloody (laughs) and we'd bring 'em in about midnight and clean up the legs and have frog leg feast at midnight—pretty good eatin'.

Note:

Dad might have been the boss, but my uncle Shelby got known as "fivesacks" because he was able to carry five 90-pound sacks of cement at once!

Look at all the lovers

runnin' from their past

Gassin' up just to get somewhere

goin' nowhere fast

Highways and heartaches

go together like you and me

Do you ever think about it

when the night is sad and lonely?

Joe Ely
Highways and Heartaches

Long And Lonely Night
A Song Of The Road

FOLK MUSIC is filled with road songs and most traveling musicians have written at least one. So it makes sense that on this given day I would write a road song—a desert road song that is sad and lonely. Certainly the terrain that we drove on today was filled with plenty of inspiration for this mood.

We began driving east beneath the "ancient rim" to Burns. So just what is the ancient rim? Why do the two lakes we passed as we leave Lakeview support no fish? I had often thought about how these lakes might look different were they fresh-water lakes. They would be surrounded by houses and cabins, the way all lakes are. But these lakes, Abet and Summer, are alkali lakes. In other words, they are filled with salt. Nothing can survive in them except a certain type of brine shrimp, which makes them an important stop on the migration trail for shore birds, especially the Snowy Plover.

Lakes Abert and Summer were created by the demise of the Pleistocene era fresh-water lake, Lake Chewaucan. As it declined, the alkali and salt were concentrated into these bodies of water. There is a small trickle of fresh water that comes in from the Chewaucan river. But the lakes, though beautiful, are bare. They are surrounded by the golden, rolling hills typical of Central Oregon. In this particular region, the hills are almost devoid of foliage, except for very sparse amount of sagebrush. Hovering over it all is the Abert Rim, a very steep rise that looms 2500 feet above the lake.

As we traveled through this barren landscape, I wondered if today's song inspiration would come from here. I briefly thought about a song called *Abert Lake:*

> A few miles out of Lakeview, beneath the ancient rim,
> Lies a little lake where fish will never swim.

No. that didn't do anything for me. Nothing came to mind, and the alkali lakes would not be my inspiration.

[But I wondered briefly if at some time in the distant past a more unsuspecting traveler, parched from the long journey across the desert might have stumbled upon this lake and at first been delighted, ready to quench his horse's thirst, only to find that there would be no sustenance there.]

We are a restless country. We began with a relentless migration from across the seas and continued with our migration across a vast and uncharted territory known as America. First we traveled by horseback, wagon, train, boat and then eventually by automobile.

Dad's own youthful journey came to mind and the songs of the dustbowl written by Woody Guthrie in particular. In his song, "Dust Storm Disaster," Guthrie writes:

> We loaded our jalopies
> and piled our families in,
> we rattled down that highway
> to never come back again.

As we traveled, I opened up my brain like I might lift a window sash and welcomed in the creative impulses. What came was not a song of my dad's journey past but of the journey present and of my own journey.

There was still a certain pull in my heart for the state of birth where I spent the first 13 years of my life and for the Pacific Northwest to where I was transplanted as a teenager. I have aunts, uncles, and cousins in the Sacramento Valley and visit there regularly. My immediate family resides now in Oregon and Washington, and I have high school and college friends I visit when I return.

It was that nostalgia I was feeling as we drive today. Since we would be in the car awhile, it seemed obvious to me that this day's songwriting inspiration would come during the trip. Once we got to my brother's place there wouldn't be much time for thought.

We drove along in silence, having exhausted the topic of Dad's southern migration. He lifted a finger to point and made some observations. As we passed the town of Wagontire, (Population 2) he said, *"Jack and Ann Peila (my brother's in-laws) started in this area. They owned that store. Jack owns all of this land. Brings his cattle here in the summer to graze."*

I had heard this story, so I was able to listen with one ear, letting mind drift while humming under my breath.

> The road—endless.
> The landscape—bare, except for sagebrush.
> The mountains—few and distant.

All this contrived to create my own road song: "Long and Lonely Night. " The song is a series of images focusing on the desert. I think it is only natural that a bleak desert landscape should conjure up a sense of loneliness and that loneliness should relate itself to a lost romance.

I had been gone from the Northwest for 30 years. As we drove along, I tried to people my mind with the memories of those I once knew. I imagined coming home and seeing how they've changed.

The final stanza of today's song says:

Your face is in my memory as I cruise into town
and I wonder if I'll see you there, parading up and down
with your cowboy hat and cowboy boots and your lovely wife
and I wonder if I'll see you there
throughout a long and lonely life.

Was there anyone in particular I was thinking? No, it just was the right way to end this song. My friend Steve Gilligan (who plays bass guitar on the CD) said that when his wife Mary heard the ending she said, "Oh, that's so sad." I think she found it a bit of a surprise. There was no hint early on in the song about this particular ending, only a hint in each chorus that the singer is lonely. But then, that is one type of songwriting at its best I think—when we surprise the listener.

Jerry and Daryl at Daryl's place in Burns, Oregon

78

Long and Lonely Night

The black line stretches out ahead—seems to go on and on.
All I can do is follow 'til the end.
One mountain guards the barren land—a silent sentinel.
It seems to lean towards me like a friend.
I start to count the sagebrush that lines the old highway
and all I do is think of you, the long and lonely day.
The sun melts into distance and takes the clear blue sky.
There's not much I can do but watch it go.
Beneath my engine's purring hum I hear coyotes cry;
the desert's eyes are watching me I know.
One by one the twinkling stars casts a misty light
and all I do is think of you the long and lonely night.
This land's been here forever and it makes me feel so small;
I wonder if there's anyone who cares for me at all.
There's something in the starkness that gets into my mind—
makes me think of you, the love I left behind.
Your face is in my memory as I cruise into town;
I wonder if I'll see you there, parading up and down
with your cowboy hat and cowboy boots
and your lovely wife,
and I wonder if I'll see you there
throughout a long and lonely life.
The black line stretches out ahead
—seems to go on and on.

Dear Okie, if you see Arkie
Tell 'im Tex got a job for him out in Californy
Pickin' up prunes, squeezin' oil out of olives
Dear Okie, if you see Arkie
Tell 'im Tex got a job for him out in Californy
Rakin' up gold, playing fiddle in the Follies
Now, he'll be lucky if he finds a place to live
But there's orange juice fountains flowing
for those kids of his.

(Rudy Sooter / Doye O'Dell)

A folk song is what's wrong
and how to fix it or it could be
who's hungry and where their mouth is or
who's out of work and where the job is or
who's broke and where the money is or
who's carrying a gun and where the peace is.

Woody Guthrie

Woody Guthrie — Dust Bowl Troubadour

The most well-known and influential of all songwriters during the time of the Great Depression was Woody Guthrie.

Guthrie was born 13 years before my Dad and so was that much older when he became known as "The Dust Bowl Troubadour" because of the many songs he wrote and performed concerning the plight of those affected.

My friend, Howie Rashba, pediatrician by day and folksinger by night, reminded me of a coincidence. Not only was Guthrie aligned with my father through geographical birthright, he also journeyed to the Pacific Northwest and was commissioned to write songs for the Bonneville Power Administration in Washington State for an intended documentary. Howie could not help but see a link between Woody's life, Jerry Ross's life, and this book. Both Woody and Jerry left the impoverished South for California—both ended up in the Pacific Northwest at some time, and Jerry's daughter would eventually take on a challenge to write a song a day while traveling in the North Country.

Granted, the resemblance is tenuous. My seven songs in seven days cannot begin to compare with the 26 songs that Woody wrote during his 30 days with the BPA, songs that included "Roll On, Columbia Roll On" and "Pastures of Plenty." Also, Guthrie's *Dust Bowl Songs* chronicle a hard time that my Dad does not think he had. In folk music, Woody is revered as an activist folksinger. He had this to say about his music:

"I hate a song that makes you think that you are not any good. I hate a song that makes you think that you are just born to lose . . . I am out to fight those songs to my very last breath of air and my last drop of blood. I am out to sing songs that will prove to you that this is your world and that if it has hit you pretty hard and knocked you for a dozen loops, no matter what color, what size you are, how you are built. I am out to sing the songs that make you take pride in yourself and in your work."

Jerry at work

After I left high school, I just started looking for work—you worked at whatever came up and whatever suited you. I started out doing shop work, fixing hop machines and working in the hops. They were quite a crop then. Went home and gave my paycheck to Mom. I guess I always wanted to be a cowboy. The first moving picture show I saw was Tom Mix, and me and JT and Gilbert always used to play cowboy.

Jerry Ross

Work

THE DAY WAS HOT as we drove to Silver Lake. Dad's old pickup didn't have any air conditioning so the windows were rolled down, and Dad drove comfortably, one-handedly, his elbow resting against the window frame. He flaunted Oregon seat belt laws and refused to wear one. (If we went through a town he pulled it over his shoulder). I looked at his sturdy, calm profile, relaxed and looking as he always did when behind the wheel, as if it were one of the most natural places on earth for him to be.

The short time at my brother's had been very enjoyable and before the party, I received the tour of the new things that Daryl had done to his place. Fences, barns, stonework—he had done it all himself.

"How did you learn to do all of this Daryl?" I asked him. "I don't remember Dad actually teaching any of you boys how to do the things you do."

"No, he just went about his work and we absorbed it somehow. I just figure I can do it, and go about doing so. I can't see paying someone to do something I can do myself."

It seems to me that is the Ross way. I did the same thing when I decided I could learn electrical wiring when we built our first house. I remember my dad telling me once his philosophy about trying new things: "I figure that 'so and so' can do it, and he's an idiot, so I figure I can do it. "

You can get away with saying things like that when you're a cowboy.

It prompted me to ask Dad to tell me about the jobs he had, because I had heard bits and pieces about all of his different occupations. It always amazed me that he seemed to find something he could do, or learn to do something he wanted to do. He certainly wasn't afraid to try. If he could boss around his elders at the age of 16, I guess he could do about anything. We left Daryl's drive, turned right on Highway 20, drove through Burns, and headed out on Highway 395 back the way we had come in. As the morning sun warmed the cool desert air I settled back, very happy to let my dad take me with him as he worked is way through California in the mid-twentieth century.

WORKING THE RODEOS

After we finished up working at Camp Beale and I was about 18, I went to work in the rodeo. Slim Pickens (the actor) was just starting out. He was a great big old kid, and he had a little black mule that he rode around in the arena. He had a cape and he'd call himself El Toreador Bullfighter. He was just a kid out of Oklahoma, but he went along to be an actor—made a lot of movies, guest-starred in Bonanza a lot of times. He really didn't have to act, just be himself, act natural, he fit in that way. He drove a lot of stagecoaches in those movies. He could handle a six-up easily. He bought a big ranch in Idaho and it's been about 15 years since he died—died fairly young.

Well he would get out and fight bulls, and I'd get out there and help him. It wasn't like it is now because they didn't have Brahmas, just Herefords, but they would come at you.

I worked in the rodeo summers from 1941–1945. Wild cow milking, bareback and bull riding. That's when I met old Bill Carli. I mugged for him while he roped. Later on, I'd meet up with his brother Louis and then finally met old Julius Carli and we became good friends.

MAKING BARRELS

Kinda at the same time, I went to coopering with Chris Magee. He owned that Dillard store there, he and his wife, and he was a cooper by trade and we'd go to all of the wineries and build redwood barrels;

they was just like a oak barrel but they would be about 36 foot in diameter and 20 feet tall and hold about 70,000 gallons.

One time, he got a contract to go down to the Gold Globe beer brewery in San Francisco, and they had a bunch of redwood tanks up and they was wanting 'em torn down and got rid of so they could go into the stainless steel and we went down there and tore those down. And we went over to Santa Rosa and that country, there was a lot of big wineries up there—Swiss Colony that was one of the biggest there was—working in those redwood tanks. That's where they'd put that wine to age in those wooden tanks and they'd form about one inch of cream of tartar and they'd chip that cream of tartar off and sell it and that's what you get in them spice jars.

When you put the barrels together (they are pre- cut when they come there) the circle is the bottom, and you beat them together with a wooden mallet, and then the staves are crow cut and fit the edge of the circle all around and they're tapered just like the old oaken barrels that they put whiskey in, and when you put your tulle in and mix that with flaxseed meal—that'd make it pretty tight so it wouldn't leak. You had a four foot lathe and as you stood up, you'd take a shingle nail and you'd drive it into the staves. Then as you went around, a contour like that would make the container stand up and it wouldn't fall.

We nailed 'em all the way around and then we'd put the top together just like the bottom and drop that onto the top crows. Then we'd measure it, and I think at that time we were looking for 18" shrinkage; when you'd drive, everyone would hit at the same time, and it would knock that down each time you hit it. About six of us would get on top of the barrel and drive the top down. We'd drive the hook around about a foot. You'd just keep walking round and round until you'd reach the bottom, then you'd cut another one and you'd put that in the middle. The flat bars would come in lengths and you'd cut the holes in the bars.

Dad halted his narrative as we pulled into the town of Riley and to the little truckstop just west of Burns where Highway 395 intersects with US 20. We decided to gas up here and I went into the little store for a paper cup of coffee. We still had a ways to go before we got to Silver Lake, and I figured I'd need it. Dad sat in the cab while the attendant came out to fill the tank, (you can't pump your own in Oregon) and I could see him chatting with the young woman who came out to fill us up. He was always able to strike up a conversation with anyone.

I hopped back in the pick up, and Dad steered us back onto the highway.

"You were telling me about hops Dad. Was that something everyone was growing? Is that why you were working in them?" I asked.

THE HOP FIELDS

Oh yeah, there was quite a demand for hops back then. But it was costly to plant 20-foot trellis and all that wire, so they were an expensive crop to raise. In order to raise hops, you would have to get an advance, (mostly Jews were the buyers and they'd give an advance) but they were a good money crop in their heyday.

When I first started in the hops, I farmed for the Carli's. They had 20 acres of hops; I used horses and hand-pickers—the hand pickers got one dollar a pound and would, if lucky, get a hundred pounds a day so they'd make about$100 a day.

I'd get up about 4 a.m., and I'd take an old Chevy truck with bows and canvas over it and benches in it and go down to Sacramento and pick up a whole load of hand- pickers off of Second Street where the winos were, and a lot of them were winos, and I'd haul 'em out to pick hops all day and I'd pay 'em off in cash and then bring 'em back at night.

And you had to watch 'em—they'd pick up stems and such and you'd stay by the truck and watch 'em while they dumped them and dock 'em if there was too much trash; they would stick a lot of leaves and stems to make them heavier. The hop itself don't weigh much but the pollen in it was what they were after.

All through high school I worked for Julius Carli's brothers, Louis and Bill Carli, running harvesters and hauling out sacks of grain at harvest time. Machine pickers for the hops came in about a year after I started working in them.We had to have extra help at harvest time even after we got the machines though; we didn't need a bunch of hand pickers, but we did need about 10–12 men to do the hand work of tying the strings in the hops and grubbing 'em and helping unload the machines when we picked. You couldn't find people who wanted to do hand labor anymore so we'd get braceros; they were all green card; it was all legal. They were brought in by the US government (from Mexico) *because labor was short after the war.*

You had to provide a bunkhouse for them and we'd get a new bunch every year; they were a pretty good bunch of guys. You could tell the good workers. If they were wearing sandals that had been half-soled with a piece of old car rubber they were good, if they were wearing American shoes, they had been there before; they'd cheat on you— they knew the score. I got along real good with the Mexicans; they liked me. I could speak a little of their lingo, and they wanted to learn English. They'd trade you word for word; they wanted to learn. Old Carli and me were just getting some horses in then, and some of those young Mexican kids were good horsemen; old Carli would start quizzing 'em about what they knew about horses but it was against the law to put 'em on a horse; every once in a while we'd get a kid who was really good.

One year there was a kid that Carli let work on the colts—we had one big Palomino filly— a two year old. He'd let him start riding it and in about three weeks he was completely broke. That kid was standing up in the saddle twirling a rope around that colt.

I interrupted for a minute. "I remember visiting in the hops. I was fascinated by the big dryers. I could walk in and look down at all of those hops in the huge bins."

That would have been down at Ledbetter's 'cause I helped him out too. He had a picking machine. Portable machines. Cecil Miller made those. They were the first mechanical picking machines. They were on two wheels and had a tongue, and you set them on the back of a Caterpillar and pulled them through. You'd have four men on the back of the Cat and two on top in the crow's nest who jerked the vine off the wire that was tied and dropped the ends down. The two on the road would push it back through the machine and little fingers would pull off the hops. We couldn't use the braceros for that, because they weren't allowed to be on machines. Ledbetter had one and George Brooks had one, and Carli had one.

There was a lot wrong with the way Cecil Miller made those things, so T Campbell and I worked on those machines day and night so that they would pick better, do a better job. And then we'd keep 'em running during hop time. The hops along Deer Creek were earlier than those over at Napa and that country and after we'd get through pickin' down there you could pull those machines behind a truck, so we'd pull 'em over to Napa and pick their hops. And that was quite an experience and

87

that's how we got real good. Then the stationary machines came out and they were kind of a messed up deal too and so we worked on them a lot and revised them because we knew hops and the people who built 'em didn't. We got quite a name in specialist hop machines and we got a call from them up at Napa and wondered if we'd come up and keep their machines running. T and I went up—T had just bought a '51 pickup so we went up in that—and they gave us $100 a day apiece and that was a lot of money then and we'd work day and night on those things but we'd keep 'em running.

We had to dry hops down to about 14% to prevent mold. The kilns were about 20 foot high and they had slats in the bottom with burlap over them and underneath them there were pipes carrying heat under 'em and at the top they were built with a cupola that had a big fan and that drew the heat up through the hops and that dried 'em. I did that once at one hop field. I ran the dryers at night and kept them going.

DRIVING TRUCK

Dad seemed to be in a talking mood, so I urged him on. "When did you do that trucking business with Claude, Dad?" One of my dad's long time friends was Claude Ballew. Claude was a few years older than Dad, but they had met through one of Dad's old girlfriends and hit it off. As short and dark as Dad was tall and fair, Claude shared my dad's sense of fun and adventure and love of horses and machinery. They teamed up with my grandpa's old truck to haul fence posts down from the hills and sell them in Galt. They did that for awhile and then got the chance at something bigger.

That was in 1944 or 5, (I was about 20) we bought an old Peterbilt truck and trailer and we'd haul a lot of lumber up to those lumber mills. We'd get a load of lumber and take it down to the Bay area and we'd try to get a load of something else to bring back. We did OK, but we had to stay up long hours.

What ended it was Claude—there was this narrow gauge railroad with no wigwags on the road and Claude was comin' to the crossing and went and dozed off, driving ok, but the train saw he wasn't going to stop and they whistled and it woke him up and he started to twist it and it hit the 3rd rail and tore it out and the electricity was flying around and when it came to a stop he jumped out; he flung himself out and missed the volts, but tore the truck all to pieces and they had to haul it away. By the time they fixed it, we were doing something else and that ended truckin'.

WE TRAVELED 162 miles to Silver Lake and for 134 miles of that, there was nothing but the muted tones of sage and sand meeting an unbelievably blue sky. Just a short while after we left Riley, I noticed a lone mountain rising out of the desert landscape. "What mountain is that, Dad?"

"The locals around here called that 'Squaw Tit Mountain' until someone got upset. I don't know what the real name is. I guess that's not what they call 'politically correct' is it?" He laughed.

"No dad, not really." I shook my head. But political correctness is not part of the West where toponomy is concerned. (I was reminded of a book I read called *From Squaw Tit to Whorehouse Meadow*, by Mark Momonier. It discusses where place names come from. The subtitle is "How maps name, claim, and inflame." Names involving racial slurs, perjoratives, and body parts are much more common west of the Mississippi than east of it as you might imagine. But Oregon has more places named "Squaw" than any other state (44), and there is a movement afoot to replace this word with acceptable tribal names. The more appropriate name for this mountain is Paiute Butte.)

The only interruption in this leg of US 395 was the little "town" of Wagontire that we had passed on our way to Burns the previous day. It appeared out of the empty desert like a mirage. Wagontire consists of a gas station, cafe, motel, general store, recreational vehicle park and, across the road, a dirt runway and windsock labeled with a sign: Wagontire International Airport. I remembered the airport sign. I had seen it often and asked about it. "Do planes land here Dad?"

"Oh, yeah, it's a real landing strip; but the international part is about as real as the sign on the café that says "town hall." But the café is pretty good. Stopped there a few times."

Wagontire behind us, we continued on down the road, still quite a distance from our destination.

"So Dad, what did you do after trucking?" I asked, ready to resume the stories.

THE RICE FIELDS

WELL, I HAD BEEN GOING up the rice fields every fall and running the combines only during harvest, but then the Willys approached me to come work for them steady. By this time I was married, so I said if they built me a house I'd come work for them. He said how 'bout we give you the materials and you build your own house? I said, that'd work. So, that's what they did. I hired T Campbell; we'd been working together. He had a little shop in town and we'd been working on cars, and machinery and carpentry. And so I hired him, and he came up with me, and he and I built us a house up there and we started working for the Willys steady.

One winter after we moved up to the rice fields, the Sacramento River flooded and broke its banks. The Auburn ravine was up above us—it was a waste ravine. With rice you have to have water flowing so it wouldn't get stagnant and it would drain out into those canals and into the Sacramento River. That ravine got flooded under about 10 feet of water, and we were afraid that it was gonna bust those levees and come down into our district.

So we started by taking some precautions. It took me about a week to pump all the rice out of the dryers and those big concrete bins that we had, so in case the water did come in it wouldn't spoil the rice.

Next, we went up top to see if we could help those up there keep that levee from breaking. I took a horse up and rode back and forth on that ravine all night for quite a few nights without much sleep just to keep an eye on how high that water was gettin'. Finally, they decided that they'd better go back up above that levee a little ways and blow the levee back into the river so that water could drain that district up there because the houses up there were flooded, and the drain bins were flooded, and the trails were flooded, and cows were stranded on high places.

So, first thing we needed was to get an old army landing barge and build a corral on top of it and motor out to where the cows were. We made a portable chute and drove the cows up the chute and onto the landing barge. Then we'd dump them out on the dry levee so they could feed 'em. When we got em all out they decided to take them down river to our district where there was pasture and it wasn't flooded.

Also in danger were large galvanized steel Butler bins that were filled with a grain sorghum called Milo. The farmers had got paid for it by their insurance, but their insurance companies said they could have that grain if they could get it out. Someone got the bright idea to get the grain and run it through our dryer and use it for cattle feed, so we took the old landing barge and put a dump truck on it and instead of a solid gate we put a screen and we put a slush pump on there and we'd drive down over the top of those bins and stick that hose into there and we'd suck that Milo up into that truck, water and all.

The water would go out the back end and the grain would stay there, and we'd haul it into the dryer at the rice farm I'd worked for; I run the dryer and dried it out and they sold it for stock feed. It was good. It smelled pretty sour when it come in, but it wasn't germinated yet so it was solid. So I run tons and tons through that dryer and they salvaged that and got a little money, more than if they'd a sold it right after they harvested it.

The farmers wanted to blow that levee, and the Army Corps of Engineers had been called but hadn't gotten there. Folks was getting kinda antsy, so they wanted to know if anyone could set dynamite. I said yeah I can set dynamite so I was elected to blow that levee which was as illegal as it could be. Anyway they said they'd stand by me if I'd blow it, so I went down and I set charges in there. I set about ten charges, lit the fuse, and we went and jumped in a boat and got out of there fast. When it blew, the center didn't blow enough and it left an island and it was still only about a half as big as it should be. So, we had to take the boat and go out into the flood. We had to be careful and go right into the middle of the gap, because the water was rushing down each side and we could have been washed away from the island and that's where we had to get.

So we got to the island and I set more charges and we jumped in that boat and headed out of there and it seemed like it took 100 years to get away from that blow. But we did and it blew; it took about a week but it got that water out of there and we didn't get flooded. I don't know—I never did hear from anyone about using the dynamite— nothing from the Army Corps of Engineers, but the ranchers all around there thought I was pretty good.

I learned about dynamite up at Grandpa Hobday's house and up in the mining too. Those tailing piles were pretty sticky with lime, and I'd set charges in there. Old Peter Stamp, the Russian I was working with, taught me how to mash the caps into it and set the fuse. There's really not a whole bunch to it, just so's you give it enough fuse so as to get away from it before it blows, or not hammer that fuse. Actually we didn't have a tool to mash it with so you'd use your teeth — that could a blown your whole mouth open, so you did have to be careful.

Down around the country at your Grandpa Hobday's, as well as in Alta Mesa, they had those centrifugal pumps (CF) and a CF will pull water about 27 feet, but as years went on and everyone started putting them in, the water level started to drop. So the CF wouldn't work so they had to start diggin' holes to lower the pump to be close to the water. I helped Helen's dad and my dad lower theirs. The last time it was lowered it was about 25 feet and Pop wanted to go another three foot, so I climbed down in the well, then bore a hole and put about three charges of dynamite with a fuse in them, and caps and tied 'em together and lit 'em up and it seemed I never could get out of there — like it took forever to crawl out of there and then I'd stand and wait for it to go off but it seemed like a lifetime gettin' away from it. Then when I blew it all loose, I'd go down with a bucket, and Pop Hobday would stay up at the top with a rope and I'd fill the buckets and he'd haul them up and dump 'em and then we'd set the pump down close to the water and it lasted another few years. It finally got so that you couldn't go any deeper with the hole without building walls for it because it might fall in on ya, and it was kind of dangerous even when we was going that. But it was hardpan country and it pretty well held its own.

CATTLEMAN

Oregon is cattle country, consuming up to 60% of the state's farm-land. Looking out the pickup window as we drove along US 395, called by some the 'lost and forlorn' federal highway I saw, amid the vast dryness, cattle grazing in the distance. Sometimes they might be lying lazily beneath the occasional tree away from the heat of the day; at other times they might be gathered in a small mass around the watering trough or a patch of grass.

A quick glance at the topography would indicate a scarcity of rain — how do these cattle get fed? The answer: it takes a lot of land. One large rancher in the area runs 2,200 cattle on 10,000 acres.

My mom had some sheet music to a song that I used to like to sing as a little girl:

"I was born to the saddle, I'll ride til I die." I found myself humming the tune under my breath, especially the part that goes, "Now some like the cities with ranches and homes, all crowded around them with no place to roam / I'll take the country, the tall prairie hay, and mountains a hundred and ten miles away."

This is the country that my dad has learned to love. It is a far cry from the Arkansas farmland he knew as a boy and the fertile California pastures he was transplanted to. I remember when he visited me in New England, he'd shake his head at the unrelenting foliage. "How do you find you find your way around out here? You can't see anything."

"Road signs, Dad. A quaint custom, but it works for us," I said, smiling. Later I took him up to the top of Temple Mountain where the 2,045 foot view overlooks several states. He felt a little better.

All of this made me think back to Dad's journey. I knew the basics but I still marveled at how it might have happened.

"Now, Dad," I ask, "how did a poor, barefoot Arkansas farm boy become a cattle rancher? How did you learn to do that?"

WELL, I HAD READ a lot of cowboy books, just natural, went to rodeos. We had an old black horse to pull our logs out with and I got to ride him over there a lot when we weren't using him to work. Your mom had horses long before I did; she always had a horse and most of them over there had horses and they'd ride half the night over that country. But we always (my cousins Gib and Don, JT and I) played Cowboys and Indians and it was always in the back of our minds to be cowboys. I guess being a cowboy was always a fantasy as long as I can remember; the first movie I ever saw, maybe the only movie I saw as a kid was Tom Mix. They brought it to the schoolhouse—it was a silent film.

Julius Carli had given me old Julie the old sway back mare. And then we had Blackie, an old Morgan mare, the one that you kids learned to ride on. Old Everett Willy had a hard time getting around from one machine to another so he bought that old mare and then when we moved he wanted to know if I wanted her. He got her from Bill Howard, a Quarter Horse man, and he was the one who brought the

Poco horses in from Texas; he brought in old Poco Willy and Poco Della and we got real acquainted and he came up to visit us in Baker and judged a show when I was President of the Quarter Horse Association there.

When we were at Arno Road, the Lombardis had cattle behind Claude's place, so I went over and started helping and got acquainted and Mr. Lombardi wanted me to work for him, and moved us up to Valley Springs in Northern California. We had to sell our place on Arno Road, so I took the job—not as much money but it was what I wanted to do. I was ready to get out of the rat race of trying to do to everything; I liked the ranching and the horses.

We were at Valley Springs (California) for a year; you went to eighth grade there, and then the Lombardis moved the ranch to Baker, Oregon. That summer before the move, we watched cattle for Lombardi up at Alpine Lake in the Sierra Mountains. That was the best time. The entire family got to come and all we did was watch cattle. Every morning we'd just saddle up, ride, and look after cattle. Lots of fun. Pretty country—you and mom and Karen would go up to the lake and go swimming in that ice water. Before he could settle in at Baker, Mr. Lombardi died, [his son] Curly had to take over and we just didn't see eye to eye. I had been with Lombardi about five years. I went on over to Keating Valley—the Steward and Morrissey ranch—for two years, then Duncans (who we went elk hunting with) made us an offer we couldn't resist and we spent a little time there. But then the Widman estate came up and the bank asked me to manage—that's how I got started with the bank. We ran that ranch for nine years. The parents on that ranch had died and left three young boys; I ran the ranch until they were able to take over. Paid off that $400,000 in inheritance tax in those 9 years.

I worked on a couple of small projects after I left Widman's. There was a ranch in Redding, California—a kind of camp for elderly people with cabins that had wheel chair access. I was down there for about eight months just after the Widman ranch. Then there was a woman in Hepner near Boardman. We helped her out for a year.

Then that trust came up at Silver Lake. Don Michael, the agribusiness man who knew me from Widman's, looked me up to run that place in '81. Silver Lake was the best ranch we ever worked because your mom got to contribute a lot more. She'd go out to ride and the

Ross kids, your cousins from Sacramento, would come up to help. It made it a nice family deal. I retired from ranching in '91; the owner wanted to sell it, and I helped the new guy who bought it and then moved to Klamath Falls and started helping everyone around there.

I got to know a lot of people at Silver Lake. I ran the Pitcher Ranch in common with Iversons, so we worked together, running cattle on BLM land, driving them out bringing 'em back.

I ran the Pitcher Ranch for about 11 years.

**Jerry's cousins Don and Gilbert, his cousin Otis, and brother JT.
They all just wanted to be cowboys.**

**The sign from The Pitcher Ranch is tacked to a tree where
Dad is living now —along with another favorite sign!**

BAKER CITY, OREGON: QUEEN OF THE INLAND EMPIRE

When I lived there, it was just Baker, a small town between the Eagle Caps and Blue Mountains. Today it is still small but is a "city." Perhaps this moniker puts it in the class of "Dodge City," that well-known Western town. Situated on The Oregon Trail, it now boasts a fine interpretive center of that time during our country's history. It was also a gold mining town and, if walls could talk, they could tell you about the seven saloons and five brothels that were housed on one block. Mothers kept their children away but the Salvation Army band would play there in the hope of reclaiming the wayward. Called the "queen of

 the inland empire," her streets are lined with history. Dad worked ranches here for 15 years. Many times he rode his horse across the famous wagon ruts that still exist from those wagons that crossed this valley all those many years ago. More than 500,000 people traveled The Oregon Trail between the years of 1840 and

1860 making it one of the most significant migrations in the history of the United States. I saw a slight irony in this situation. As an 11-year-old child, Jerry Ross took part in a significant migration. It is estimated that 1.5 million came to California from the Midwest and the South in the 1930's. Later, as an adult he spent an important part of his life on the route of another significant migration. Maybe that comes with just being a part of the West, but it seems to me to be an interesting coincidence. Baker was a big part of my life. I attended school here for five important teen years, and I received that special attention that only a small town can give. Today, when I return to visit, I am so grateful to have been here and pleased to see that the grand queen is cashing in on her Western charm and justifiably claiming her part in our country's history.

Pictured: The Historic Geiser Grand Hotel. It opened in 1889 and closed in 1963. Thirty years later, it was renovated to its former majestic splendor and reopened.

Catherine Newman Duncan
The Story Song

The Duncan Memorial in Silver Lake Cemetery

Oh, don't you remember sweet Betsy from Pike
Who crossed the wide prairie with her lover Ike.
With two yoke of oxen and one yellow dog,
A tall shanghai rooster and one spotted hog.

American Folksong

SILVER LAKE, OREGON

The sign outside of the hot dog stand in Silver Lake

TODAY WE WOULD VISIT my mother's grave and it was crossing my mind that a graveyard should be ripe with inspiration for a song. The town of Silver Lake lies in central Oregon. A sparsely populated town, it pretty much consists of the graveyard, a general store, a school, a church, and a post office. As we approached the town, Dad was full of stories and the finger pointing began. With one hand firmly on the wheel, he used the other to point areas of interest: the fence he built here or there, the mountain, "steeper 'n a cow's face" where he or some other rancher ran cattle.

He intended to have us eat lunch at The Cowboy Dinner Tree Restaurant, located between Silver Lake and Thompson Reservoir but when we arrived it was closed; so, we went back into town and bought hotdogs from the hotdog stand outside of the general store and sit down at one of the picnic tables. It wasn't long before my Dad struck up a conversation with the proprietor.

"My name's Jerry Ross. Use to run The Pitcher Ranch."

"Oh sure. I remember the name," she replied. And so they chatted about the changes since he has been gone. My Dad doesn't know any strangers and most of the day had been much the same—stopping to chat with people on different ranches we passed. They always remembered him, and he had dozens of stories to tell at every stop.

It was late afternoon as we approached The Silver Lake Cemtery—I had brought flowers for Mom's grave, curiously located in the middle of nowhere. My folks were at The Pitcher Ranch when my youngest sister died. Up to that point, they hadn't given any thought to where they might place their final remains but when this occured, my mother had to make a decision. She had purchased three plots at the Silver Lake cemetery and, when she died, she was buried next to my sister.

It was an interesting funeral. I am sure that there are not many funerals where the procession out to the graveyard is 173 miles. The funeral itself was held in Klamath Falls but then as many folks as could went out to Silver Lake. Others who could not get into Klamath Falls for the service met us at the gravesite.

The Silver Lake cemetery is larger than small but not huge. It contains well-cared-for lawns and is surrounded by a fence that separates it from the High Desert terrain. There are a few small trees by the fence but not many, and the general aspect is open and wide like it is throughout the rest of the High Desert.

After saying hello to Mom and singing a little hymn, I began to wander around looking at gravestones, waiting for that inspiration. I roamed around the cemetery looking for what might be the oldest grave. I found it in one inscribed "Catherine Newman Duncan—1881." Around her are other Duncans, particularly William Duncan, who had died several years after her. Her birthplace is labeled Kentucky, his is labeled Tennessee. I wondered what had brought these two so far from their places of birth to this lonely, small High Desert town. I glanced quickly at the monument because it was getting late and home was a few hours south of here. But on the way back, in the quiet of the pickup (my dad out of stories and me out of questions), I was able to think about the potential of this story.

There was no time to stop and do research, so I really didn't know who these Duncans were and how they came to be, so my imagination just had to tell the story as it might have been. What might have brought folks from America's southern regions to settle in this stark environment that was obviously so different from what they had known?

It certainly takes tough people to ranch this area. Dad had particularly wanted to see his old friends the Iversons, Marge and Buzzy. We sat down with Marge outside under a tree near their old farmhouse and she and Dad had a nice time remembering. Buzzy was out in the hay. They are both in their 80's. When I started thinking about Catherine and Willie Duncan, the Iversons come into my head, particularly Marge, who just embodies the strength of the pioneer matriarch. I can picture Catherine Newman ending up somewhat like her.

Like my Dad Catherine also was an immigrant, and I imagined that she had journeyed to her new home, rolled up her shirt sleeves, and dug in, as he and his family had. Through hard work, she and Willie made a home and raised their children and were finally laid to rest under the desert sky.

My mind was also on my own mother, a pioneer woman of a new age who followed her man wherever he might want to go, from a mining camp in Jackson to a weathered ranch house in the High Desert. Once a favored daughter with a piano in the parlor and her own horse, she made the transition to hardworking explorer. They were not so different, Catherine and my mom. My mother's grandmother had been one of the last to come across the country by covered wagon. The West just sizzled with stories like this. They all came West, like my dad, looking for something: land, gold, a new life. The history of Catherine Newman Duncan was just ripe to be made into a story song.

The process started clicking. This was getting fun. As Dad drove us back to Bonanza, the words just flooded my brainwaves, influenced I'm sure by old songs of pioneers I had grown up with. This was my background too. The first songs I learned to play on the guitar were the story songs like "Barbara Allen," "The Streets of Laredo," "Jesse James," and "The Old Chisolm Trail." I had always loved narrative as a girl and used to memorize entire poems like "The Highwayman" by Alfred Noyes, which is about a young lady whose love for a dashing criminal induces her to sacrifice her life to save his. Such are my influences.

The feeling is almost physical when this happens. Like Woody said, I just turn the radio dial that is in my head and let the airwaves get flooded by what I have seen. It is as if the words have a tangible presence and they are in there, 'duking it out' for supremacy and only the right ones will survive. As we drove along, the cadence came in rhythm like the clip-clop of horse hooves, telling the story of adventure and independence. The rhythm comes from the name itself: Catherine Newman Duncan. I like the name from the very beginning because of its musicality. No chorus came, just a short bridge, and after that a simple story fell out and by the time we got home, I was ready to sing it into the recorder and write it down.

Catherine Newman Duncan

Oh come along with me sweet Catherine Newman
if you've got the urge to roam,
and I'll show you things and take you places
far from your Kentucky home.
Oh her Daddy cried, "Don't you take my daughter,
she's all the world to me."
She held tight and said, "Don't listen I'm yours for eternity."
So they ran through the hills and they ran down the valleys
and into Tennessee.
He turned and said, "Sweet Catherine Newman
won't you marry me?"
"Oh, I'll marry you my wild, Willy Duncan
'cause I've got the urge to roam
if you'll show me things and take me places
far from my Kentucky home."
From the Mississippi Delta to the North Dakota plain,
they fought outlaws and wild fires and suffered torrential rains.
Panned for gold in California, fished the Puget Sound,
in good times and bad times, rambled and gambled
this country up and down.
They buried three children, had another four.
Then one day Catherine Newman Duncan said, "
I can't take no more.
Oh let's settle here my wild Willy Duncan, in this barren land
and find us a way to eke out a livin' in the juniper and sand."
It was in the High Desert country that they made their home
when Wild Willy and Catherine Newman Duncan
lost the urge to roam.
Life was hard but she put up a fight
and became a livin' legend before death put out her light.
They took her down to the outside of town
and in a February thaw, they laid her body down.
Oh what do you dream of Catherine Newman Duncan
when you hear the North Wind moan?
Are you glad that you left you feather bed
in your old Kentucky home?

Silver Lake Fire Memorial

Note:

Had I rambled around the graveyard a little more, I might have come across the memorial to the 43 people who were killed on Christmas Eve in a fire caused by the overturning of a lamp at Christman Bros. store in Silver Lake. That might have made for an interesting tragedy narrative; the bright hopes of the residents of this prosperous trading post community came crashing down with a one- gallon oil lamp and the flames spread rapidly through the rickety building. It is still considered one of the worst fire disasters in Oregon, and it took the residents a long time to recover from the shock.

(www.bowmanmuseum.org)

SILVER LAKE, OREGON FIRE, DECEMBER 24, 1894

40 ARE DEAD! Horrible Holocaust at a Holiday Fete in Oregon. OVERTURNED LAMP Sets Fire to the Hall and Escape is Cut Off. OTHERS WILL DIE. The Story of the Sad Disaster is Most Graphically Told.

ASHLAND, Ore., Dec. 29. – Advices were received here last evening from Klamath Falls, Ore., of a most horrible and fatal accident at Silver Lake, Lake County, Oregan, [sic], caused by the overturning of a lamp at a gathering on Christmas Eve, in which over forty lives were lost and sixteen persons badly injured, five of whom will probably die. The gathering had assembled in the hall above Christman Bros.' store, and consisted of children who, with their parents and relatives, were having a grand time and enjoying what Santa Claus had brought them, little dreaming that many of them would never leave the building alive.

Someone attempted to get where he could see and hear better by jumping up on a bench in the middle of the hall. In doing so, his head struck a lamp hanging from the ceiling causing the oil to run out, which immediately caught fire. While trying to take the lamp down it was tipped so that the oil ran out on the floor. From that time on, the scene was terrible. The lamp was finally taken down, but it fell to the floor. In the attempt to get it outside, it was kicked to the door, where it lay, as it could not be touched on account of the intense heat. People were compelled to rush through the flames in order to reach the door and many perished in the attempt.

The building, a two-story structure, including the Post Office and the entire stock of goods of Christman Bros., were consumed. Further particulars could not be learned last night. Silver Lake is over a hundred miles from Klamath Falls and the stage brought the news to this place.

Fort Wayne News, Fort Wayne, IN 29 Dec 1894

THE REST OF THE STORY

I found out later that the story I concocted of Catherine Newman Duncan bears little resemblance to the reality. For fun, I decided to google the name and was surprised when something actually came up.

My brief time at the cemetery, without a camera or a notepad, seems to have resulted in a factual error. Catherine Newman was married to Warren Spiller Duncan, not William as I had first thought. However, William is the family name, with the original William sailing from England. This information may have been on the gravestone, or my memory had just played tricks on me.

In an article from "The Centennial History of Oregon 1811 – 1912" Vol. 2, I learned that Warren and Catherine's daughter Louisa was born in Illinois where Warren served as Sheriff for 11 years before moving to Marion County, Iowa. He was always a farmer. Later he moved to Lane County, Oregon, just above Springfield to live with his son George Duncan, who had come to the state in 1852 (and had a lake named after him). Warren died there in 1878 at the age of 85. There is no other mention of Catherine Newman except that she died in 1881 in Paisley, Lane County, Oregon, at the age of 74. She was 19 when she married Warren, who appears to have been 34. However, it appears to be Warren M. Duncan, (not Warrenton S.) who is buried beside Catherine. This could be a son, and Warren Sr. may have outlived his young wife and been buried elsewhere. I do not know.

In 1852, Warren would have been 60 and Catherine 45. According to a plaque that I found online, they seemed to have had 10 children, not the seven that I mention in the song. And so it appeared that Wild Willy and Catherine Newman's great escape from Tennessee and Kentucky was not as romantic as I painted it (although I did have the states correct); however I liked my version a great deal. How she came to be buried in Silver Lake remains a mystery, as does how many of those children lived. Records vary as to who is buried where. That didn't really matter to the song.

I don't know what compelled a sweet young 19-year-old to marry a man 15 years her senior who was a farmer and a sheriff, but it sounded like an adventure to me!

Brush Arbor, courtesy of the Latibah Collard Museum

Imagine for a moment walking toward an outdoor meeting being held in your community. As you walk up into an open field you see in the distance a rustic shelter and coming from that place you hear the strains of "When The Roll Is Called Up Yonder" being played upon stringed instruments or a pump organ that has been brought by wagon. A large crowd is gathering beneath bows of greenery that block out the sun, giving the place a yellow-green color as the branches filter the light. A slight breeze wafts across the crowd on this hot summer day as you find a place to sit on one of the long benches that were hastily constructed for the meeting. You can't help tapping your foot to the sound of the music as everyone anticipates what is to come because you have just entered a brush arbor meeting.

Pamy Blaine, *Openwriting.com*

Religion

ON SUNDAY MORNING, Dad and I rose and had our coffee as usual. He got up occasionally to tend to some beans he had placed in his crock-pot in preparation for the potluck at the Klamath Falls Baptist Church.

Much of my early life was centered around the Cypress Missionary Baptist Church on Bradshaw Road in Sacramento, California. We have old home movies that showed my family piling into the old Volkswagen bus one Easter. In them we were dressed in our finest—suit coats for the boys and new dresses and hats for us girls. I seemed to have had a little difficulty making the high step into the van in my tight skirt. That video reinforced a specific memory, however the other memories were less specific but still clear; they had just merged into one memory—vacation Bible schools, Sunday School, singing hymns, a singing trio with my sister Karen and cousin Terri, potlucks, church suppers, and picnics. Every Sunday morning and Sunday evening had found us there. There was a large Ross contingent. My dad's brother JT and his family and his sister Drothey and her family both attended; Grandma Emma was a founding member. The three siblings generated 14 children between them, and church was almost an extension of our family.

Church continued to play an important part in my dad's life, and I could see he was eager to leave.

"When do you want to go dad?" I asked.

"Oh, it's about 45 minutes away, so I guess we'll leave about 9."

It was only about 8 a.m., so we had enough time for a relaxed chat before leaving.

"What do you remember, Dad, about going to church when you were a kid in Arkansas? Did everybody go? What was it like?"

He was not sitting as usual but was moving slowly about the kitchen, putting the last touches on his beans.

"Religion—well that was just something everybody did. You were born that way. Everybody in the country went to church. You were raised with that initiative—you just inherited it I guess. A lot of people changed when they were older, but most followed the same path."

"You'd go out into the woods and build a church?"

"Yep. I guess no one had the money to build a permanent building and that way they could choose a central location for a lot of families."

That certainly was in keeping with the philosophy with which I was raised. A church was not a building but rather it was a group of people who shared beliefs and values and daily live the tenants of their faith. The group of people who made up the small congregation at Klamath Falls certainly met this description.

Dad liked to get there early, so I usually got to greet the congregation individually as they arrived. They were always cordial and very happy to have me there. I was usually encouraged to sing something, either in a duet or solo, which my dad always liked. Because of the many members who, like my father as a child, travel a great distance, this church had taken to combining the standard morning and evening services into one service that was separated by a potluck lunch.

I took my dad's beans downstairs to the kitchen and chatted briefly with Norma Northcutt and her daughter-in-law Shelly, who were setting things up.

"It's so nice to see you!" Norma said.

"Are you staying long?" Shelly asked.

"Actually, I am on my way out today," I said. "I have to cut my trip a little short this year because I was doing an overnight fundraising walk in Seattle, which shortened my time here."

"Oh, that's right. I remember. The walk for suicide prevention, in memory of your sister." Shelly cut a tray of brownies into squares and put them on a tray. "How was that?"

"It was really a nice time. It's almost spiritual, walking overnight like that. It was especially nice walking along Puget Sound at dusk."

"I'll bet," said Norma. "I love Seattle. Well, we're sorry you can't stay longer. How's your dad doing? Is he still having those headaches?"

"Yes, I think so, but he doesn't complain much. You know, I wish he could get a second opinion—maybe from a specialist."

"Well, there isn't a whole lot his P.A. out there in Bonanza doesn't know; he's been doing this a long time. He's good. But, if it will make you feel better, we can see that he talks to someone else," Norma reassured me.

Both Shelly and Norma later saw to it that dad visited another doctor, and Shelly made sure she stayed with him and asked all of the right questions. It was such a relief to me to know that they were there. They were the best. Friends. Church people.

FAITH OF OUR FATHERS

Historians of the American twentieth century are just beginning to think productively about religion. Apart from the dedicated specialists, the historical profession has routinely sidelined this rich and complicated subject, passing off references to religious institutions and belief systems quickly, paying close attention only when faith becomes forcefully politicised as it did during the fundamentalist struggles of the 1920's and in the culture wars of the late twentieth century. That is a mistake. Religion matters. The churches that relocated southerners built would affect the entire landscape of faith and also the landscape of politics in the places they settled.

(Gregory 197)

One thing that defined my family as they journeyed from Arkansas to California was their faith. The combination of faith with work ethic and family loyalty almost ensured their success.

The Southern emigrants did not go to California as shallow beings, uncertain and rootless, succumbing to the overwhelming tide of the Depression. In addition to their rural heritage and family, they brought with them their religious faith, and the churches they built would affect the areas they settled. While they struggled to make ends meet, religion was the glue that held them together, satisfied the soul, and was the reason for everything. All things mysterious and unexplained were in God's hands.

I knew that my Grandma Emma had never wavered in the beliefs that kept her going into her 80's. Our family has a record of the testimony she gave for the homecoming of Cypress Missionary Baptist Church, and it gives insight into the faith that the travelling Southerners brought with them into California. Certainly, one wonders if, without this faith, those who journeyed would have survived at all.

TESTIMONY (EXCERPT) OF EMMA ROSS, APRIL 1980
CYPRESS MISSIONARY BAPTIST CHURCH HOMECOMING

I have been around a long time, as you can see. I was born in Ozark County, Missouri, 76 years ago into a Christian home. I was saved at an early age. I married a Missionary Baptist boy. I recall before we were married he was sent as a messenger to the Association. He had to pass by our place and he stopped to say hi. He was riding a mule—that was in 1920. Times have changed since then, I'm afraid, not for the better but for the worst. One thing for sure—human nature hasn't changed. After I was saved, I was baptized by the Freewill Baptist Church, and it took me a long time to realize I needed scriptural Baptism. It was during a revival Bro. Ben Crawford was holding at Hagginwood. I asked him to preach on baptism. He said it was one of his favorite subjects. I was baptized along with my daughter, Drothey, and daughter-in-law, Helen, by the Hagginwood Church, Bro. Hubbard, pastor. We were driving to church all the way from Alta Mesa, to quite a ways beyond Wilton. Finally, a sign went up in front of that old Japanese schoolhouse down the road which said Missionary Baptist Church. We decided to visit. After we visited a few times, we decided to join. We were few in number, but everyone was so friendly and nice—they made us feel right at home. If I were to write all that has happened in those 28 or more years, it would fill a book. God has really blessed. It takes a people that have a mind to work and give of their time and money. I have 17 grandchildren. I think the greatest highlight for me is they are all saved—and 13 of them were saved here, and baptized by this church. This all started when I fell in love and married a man who was on his way to the Association, riding a mule.

Pictured: Emma Freeman Ross and Ralph Ernest Ross

Church People

A Song Of Thanks

Cypress Missionary Baptist Church, Sacramento, California (1950's)

Come to the church in the wildwood,

Oh, come to the church in the vale;

No spot is so dear to my childhood

As the little brown church in the vale.

William S. Pitts, 1857

WHEN I LEFT KLAMATH FALLS after my visits home, I always departed on a Sunday; I went to church with Dad, and then I had him drop me off at the airport after.

Earlier that morning, I had thought that I would end up with a gospel tune for today's song. That would seem the normal progression of things given that I had just left a church service. But no gospel tune came; instead I felt only a great deal of thanks for the church—that little group of people who had been so instrumental in the lives of my parents.

My mom was the one who was the consistent churchgoer through the years. She was not actually raised Baptist but became one when she married my father. Daddy was raised in the church but sometimes found reasons not to attend—usually related to some aspect of farming. But Mom would make sure that her six children were out of bed, scrubbed, and dressed in their best clothes in time to make it to Sunday School. That didn't mean that my Dad was not a firm believer because he was and is. But the activity of the actual service did not mean as much to him as it did to my mother at that time.

Dad and JT helped build the church building, however, it is of course, a community that defines a church. My mom felt the need for a church community and always sought out the nearest Missionary Baptist church. When the folks retired and moved to Bonanza, Oregon my mother immediately looked for a church. She found a church home in the Klamath Falls Missionary Baptist Church.

In this church there is a painting that provides the backdrop for the baptistery where souls are born again to hymns of joy and shouts of hallelujah. It is a lovely, lush, restful scene—a river, trees, and blue sky. My mother painted it while in the last throes of Parkinson's disease. She hadn't painted for years, her hands unsteady, her balance unsure. But then they asked, "Will you paint us one Helen?" Dad remembers getting up late in the night to find her in her studio, brush in hand, working feverishly, somehow finding the steadiness. Now that she is gone, it remains—a tribute to her inner beauty and her strong belief in a force stronger than all of us.

On this day I thought of this little church. I remembered how when she was needed, my mother would rise and slowly head to the piano, how the congregation would wait until she had settled herself unsteadily on the piano stool, and pounded out "Shall We Gather at the River" missing notes, her fingers stiff from disease. And I remembered how when she was finished, those voices would raise themselves in a loud "Amen!" One time the pastor, Ed Keady, winked at me and said, "If we keep her busy, she'll be with us longer."

I also reflected on how these church members watched over my dad after she had gone. If he were to miss a Sunday, most likely Paul Northcutt would call to see if he was all right. It relieved my mind to know that he has such friends nearby.

THE FLIGHT TO PORTLAND, OREGON, left about 4:30, so I had some time to kill. I took a short walk outside of the airport at first. As I walked (movement seemed to be key to my writing), an idea for the day's started to take shape. All of the images of the morning, the friends, the food, my mother's painting in the baptistery, were all fresh in my mind. The song began to gel. I went inside the small terminal and found myself a little cubicle, opened up the laptop, and began to write.

The song came fairly fast and was mostly finished by the time I arrived at the Portland airport. The images I drew on are obvious—they were from my past. The details were real and therefore easy to use as illustrations. Again, the melody was created by the lyrics. These lyrics require a certain tempo and type of melody—this was not a ballad. I decided there was a gospel influence after all—an old time gospel cadence was where I was going. The terminal was empty so I could hum a little. I tapped my foot. Over and over the song imprinted itself in my mind and by the time I reached the Portland airport, about six hours later, I was ready to sing it into my little recording device.

Church People

Oh there's nothing like church people
when you're feeling blue.
It's nice to know so many folk will say a prayer for you.
And when the sorrows of this world bring you to your knees
there's nothing that will lift you like that love so full and free.
When I was a little girl, I sat on Daddy's knee.
He put on my little white socks and shiny shoes for me.
And in that old, oaken pew, Mama took my hand
and traced my fingers on the notes
as we sang of "Beulah Land."
And when my Mama became ill, and she could not stand
it was those church people who lent a helping hand.
And when she died and left my Daddy all alone,
church people helped him heal his heart and keep his home.
I remember Precious Memories and the way that it was sung,
in that little country church back home when I was young.
And though I've traveled far away, it still feels so grand
to gather with church people—a hymn book in my hand.

**A painting by Helen Elizabeth Hobday Ross that hangs in the
Baptistery of The Klamath Falls Missionary Baptist Church.**

[Pete] Seeger made his way carefully among
the children to the stage." A long time ago,
people didn't <u>listen</u> to music, " he said. "They
<u>made</u> music." He asked them to help him sing.
"Did any of your ever hear this song?" and he
sang, "She'll be wearing red pajamas when
she comes – scratch, scratch."
When by the end of the first chorus, no one had sung,
He stopped. "Why, I didn't hear you," he said.
"Maybe you don't like to sing?" He began playing
again and then stopped, as if interrupted by a thought.
"Maybe you're afraid to sing," he said.
Several children widened their eyes. Others stole
glances at their teachers. Possibly no grown-up had
ever asked them to sing unless it was a hymn or "The Star
Spangled Banner." More often, anyway, one had told
them to be quiet."

(Wilkinson 108)

A Singing Heritage

"DADDY, SING IT. Sing "The Boatman." Small, girlish voices clamored from the backseat of the old Chevy and Daddy was quick to comply.

"I stand beside the riverside and look into that city below," he sang, his strong tenor voice leading this gospel song and Mom, my sister Karen and me, and perhaps one of my brothers, chiming in on the tag: I stand beside (I stand beside) the riverside (the riverside).

Thus entertained, we traveled to church and elsewhere very often this way: *The Boatman, Jericho Road, Just a Closer Walk With Thee* and many other songs and hymns entertained us. Or perhaps the travelers might be just be Mom, Karen, and me, and we would urge Mom to lead us in "Because of Him" or "I've Got A Mansion" so that we could be her back-up singers and sing in three-part harmony.

This was how we passed the time whenever we would drive some-where. Blessed with this musical family, the strong singing culture of the Baptist church and augmented by degrees in literature, no doubt I had come to my songwriting inevitably. My friend, singer-songwriter Tom Smith, once chuckled at a comment I made about not having time to write a song because I was only commuting twice that week. Perhaps singing in the car as a child began my habit of writing while I drive. Certainly, music is a huge part of my memory and is also an important way through which I remember. Doing it as I travel seems almost second nature.

My young life was peppered with gospel songs and folksongs and I remember my mom, dad and uncle singing many as I grew up. I had an affinity for the story songs of Appalachia and the British Isles and taught myself to play guitar with a folksong chord book.

The song that my Dad sings on the CD that accompanies this book, "She Appeared To Be 18 Or 19 Years Old" is attributed to the 19th century, and may have had its roots in an Irish drinking song called "A Very Unfortunate Man." A similar song was recorded by Jimmy Driftwood and was called "The Warranty Deed." Other songs and stories with similar plots have shown up over the years, including the plot of an 1898 Mark Twain play.

So goes the folksong in the oral tradition. I haven't been able to find a version of this song where the lyrics are identical to my Dad's, although several versions are close. Many of the American traditional tunes came from the British Isles along with the early settlers and most evolved through the oral tradition among the Scots, Irish, and English immigrants in the Southern mountains.

Dad said that his uncle Theodore (his mother's brother) taught him this song. Undoubtedly, someone else had taught Theodore from somewhere back, each person adding or subtracting or changing words as they went. While many of the people singing these were literate, the songs still were rarely written down and there was no such thing as copyright.

Narrative songs lend themselves well to the oral tradition and were meant to be sung from memory as a means of entertainment or as a way to chronicle an event such as a war.

Although many of these songs have been collected by people such as James Child, Alan Lomax, and Jean Ritchie, folksongs can never be said to have a definitive version. A lot of the songs my dad knew fit that description.

"Hey Dad," I asked him that evening, "do you remember that song you used to sing? The one about the young man who marries a young lady, but it turns out she wasn't so young after all? You used to sing it to us when we were kids."

"Uncle Theodore taught me that song."

"Uncle Theodore was Grandma Ross's brother?"

"That's right—the youngest. He was only a few years older than Shelby and always into trouble. I remember he used to like to read those Western paperbacks—Tom Mix and such—and Grandpa Thomas didn't allow such heathenish stuff—I used to tell on him." He laughed.

"Do you think you can remember and sing the song?" I prodded.

"Well, I don't know. My voice ain't in great shape. I haven't been singing much."

"Just give it a try." I positioned the recorder where I thought it wouldn't make him nervous and encouraged him. He leaned back and closed his eyes and began to sing. His vocals were a little shaky with age, but the timbre and pitch, as well as the confidence to launch into the song a cappella, certainly gives credence to his musical background.

She Appeared to be 18 or 19 years old

As a was a walkin' down by the seashore
I spied a young lady she sure did look grand.
Her laces and diamonds, her hair shone like gold,
she appeared to be 18 or 19 years old.
And when we'd been married, retired for a rest,
my love for her changed when my love did undress.
A full box of powder my love did unfold,
she appeared to be 40 or 50 years old.
She unsnapped her fingers, I just counted three,
took off her peg leg right up to her knee.
Out on the carpet her glass eye did roll,
she appeared to be 80 or 90 years old.
She took out her false teeth I thought I would faint;
scraped from her pale cheeks a full box of paint.
Took off her false wig, her bald head did show,
I'd married an old lady 'bout 100 years old.
So boys take my warning and don't be like me
and marry the first pretty girl that you see.
They'll wed you and woo you and whoa be the day,
'cause when they undress they'll be the devil to pay.

He ended laughing.

119

"That's pretty good!" I cried. He demurred and insisted that his voice wasn't clear.

"I don't use it," he said. "Not since I was singin' down there at the church."

I liked this version of my Dad's, and it evoked memories of my childhood and illustrated the part that my Dad's playfulness had in that childhood. I was happy that he grew singing and not being told to be quiet.

Short Endings To Long Goodbyes

A Song Of Observation

AFTER I TOOK THE 75-minute flight from Klamath Falls to Portland, I usually stayed in town a night or two before heading back to New Hampshire, coming or going to see a friend or two or simply enjoying the town itself. I might browse through Powell's Books (and anyone who has been to this book city knows that you can spend a day in there easily) or ride the bus through the "fareless square" of downtown Portland and do some window-shopping. In the nice weather, it was a treat to walk down to the river and stroll through the park.

I spent only one night in Portland this time. I had been on the road awhile, and I felt the need to return home. Day Six was spent largely in airports.

I had not contacted any friends but spent the previous night writing down the words to "Church People" and humming the song into my little tape recorder. As I prepared to take the hotel shuttle back to the airport, I wondered where today's inspiration would come from. Certainly an airport is a busy place with a lot going on, so there would have to be something to observe. There are few better places for people watching than airports.

I got through security early and started roaming around. The Portland airport is a favorite of mine. I like the shops and eateries there, as well as the free WIFI. I usually stop at The Rose City Café for their "Stumptown Stew." (I just found out on my last trip there, however, that Rose City Café is no more. Sigh. I have googled "Stumptown Stew" with no luck).

It was just a half hour until my flight, and I had yet to find any inspiration for today's song. Then, suddenly I spotted it. The most poignant of all goodbyes— the soldier and his girl. This is a very romantic scenario, and I knew it will make a great song.

Reflecting all of the poignancy I felt at leaving myself was this sweet scene. He is leaving. She is staying. And in their sadness, in the sweet pathos of love and youth, I found my story. The hook came immediately:

> Wet tears on fresh, young faces,
> jet planes that take us places,
> bitter partings to sweet embraces,
> short endings to long goodbyes.

Meanwhile, I had to get in line and prepare to board. The chorus swirled around in my head over, and over and it started to wrap itself around a melody and I tried to hum it under my breath.

This was also a visual piece. Because I had the exact image in my head I could work with that—description, details—they were all there.

Once we took off, I got out my notebook and wrote it down. I prefer to sing lines to myself, rather than work with a pen and paper, however, in this case, I had no choice. (Well, I guess I had a choice but chose to not disturb my seat partners or appear slightly addled by singing to myself.)

Chicago-Midway is another airport that I like. It is smaller and more intimate than O'Hare is, and my flights always seem to leave on time from there. There are some nice little eateries as well. I landed with this new song in my head and began walking around the airport humming to myself. I passed the House of Blues store where life-sized statues of John Belushi and Dan Ackroyd draw families and photographers. I went by several times in fact as I walked and created. Finally, I did sit down, order a coffee, and pulled out the paper tablet to jot down more lyrics.

It was starting to come together, so I grabbed my little digital recorder and headed to the Ladies restroom. Luckily it was empty, and I found a stall in the furthest corner and sang softly into the recorder. The song now had a good start, and I could work with it. By the time I landed in Boston, I had the entire song written down.

Like Woody Guthrie said, "The best stuff you can sing about is what you see and if you look hard enough you can see plenty to sing about ."

Short Endings to Long Goodbyes

He's in his army khakis—
she's dressed in tight blue jeans.
To separate the two of them
would take extraordinary means.
He cradles her neck and strokes her hair,
she seems to whisper in his ear.
Maybe she's saying,
"Don't you dare not come home to me."
Wet tears on fresh young faces,
jet planes that take us places,
bitter partings to sweet embraces,
short endings to long goodbyes.
He tries to leave but she refuses to let go of his hand,
averts her eyes but seems to be willing him to stay.
He looks at her as if to plead
"This is something I don't need.
It's already hard enough on me.
I'll be back someday."
I hear a distant voice interrupt the scene.
It tells me I've a plane to catch down at Gate 15.
I turn to go but I'll take their pain.
I'll think about them now and then
because I can remember
when I was so young and so in love.
Wet tears on fresh young faces,
short endings to long goodbyes.

124

A HOME IN THE WOODS

The first home I owned (in conjunction with my husband Jack) was a 1-1/2 story house in Milford, New Hampshire. We moved to New England from Arizona, where we met, to Massachusetts where my husband is from and began the search for a home. Faced with high interest rates and a tight market, I blithely suggested to my husband, "let's build our own." Jack had some carpentry background, and I had plenty of confidence in my abilities to contribute, (justified or otherwise) so we sauntered forth into this new venture, an experience we would later label "babes in the woods."

We built this house ourselves with minimal professional help and it took us about two years. Just weeks after our first son was born, we moved in. I knew that it was the example of my dad and mom that gave me the courage to even think of such a thing. I designed the house; I

learned to do wiring and lay tile; I painted and landscaped. My dear husband undertook the major tasks of hiring and supervising the excavation, doing the framing and plumbing, and hanging and taping sheetrock. We spent alternate hours (so one of us could babysit) dipping cedar shingles in Cuprinol and nailing siding, and whenever we found a spare minute we worked feverishly on the miscellaneous.

We lived there for 23 years and have since moved on, but my heart will be forever tied to this home in New Hampshire. It was there that I raised my children and it was there I learned that my mother was dying at the very time we had decided to sell. I gave the responsibility of showing the house to my son, Nicholas, and flew out West. By the time Dad came out to visit, we were in a transitional apartment, deciding our next move.

I am disappointed that Dad never got to see this little house, because he would have appreciated his legacy. It is just like singing—no one told me that I couldn't do it.

Jane Ross Fallon

A CALIFORNIA HOME

1955—1966

Stairsteps at Arno Road
Charlie, Karen Ernie, Jane, Daryl

Home Again

THE FIRST HOME I REMEMBER was a simple house, but it was luxurious compared to where my dad was raised. Our family of six divided itself into the three bedrooms, the three boys sharing one bedroom and the three girls sharing another. Mom and Dad, of course, occupied the third.

There were two bathrooms: a small one off the boys' bedroom and a larger one that could be entered from the hall from both the master bedroom and the girls' room. The rest of the house was comprised of an eat-in kitchen, a living room, and a family room of sorts. Off of the family room was a washroom with a wringer washing machine. I remember that the central bathroom had a laundry door that opened up into the family room, and it was almost magical. I would slip through that laundry door, and into some other world of my own making.

The floors were all linoleum; we had no wall-to-wall carpeting. The front yard was spacious and just the right size for the games of hide and seek or baseball that we played in the evenings. A garage was attached to the house and created an L-shape, and within the L was a patio flanked by an open-air brick fireplace. I remember playing hopscotch on the concrete patio, drawing the form myself with chalk.

It was an idyllic childhood, I think. I had built-in playmates, a temperate climate, an outdoor lifestyle, and a garden of eden next door in the form of my Grandfather Hobday's farm.

I remember on summer days when we were young, we were allowed to walk to Grandpa's down Arno Road. My oldest brother, Charlie, would lead off, and we would walk single file, by age, down the road not more than one-quarter mile. It seemed to me that my Grandpa Hobday grew everything. I remember fruit trees: apricot, orange, pomegranate. I remember large vegetable gardens where we would go to snack after swimming when we had worked up a good appetite. Out to the gardens I'd go, sinking my teeth into a large, freshly picked green pepper.

My mother loved to swim, and with the help of her dad and my uncles, Harold and Don, a swimming pool was created. It was hand dug, free form with soft rounded sides smoothed over with concrete. A large pipe filled the pool and, in later years, my uncle Harold improvised a solar collector made of pipes and black plastic that poured heated water, warmed from the California sun, into the small pool—for, I am sure now, it was small. Harold was an inventor, and this may have been one of the earliest solar heaters. Later my mother, who was always artistic, painted on the walls of this pool; we could go underwater to see her creations of whales, octopi, fish—all that she had painted on the sides and bottom of this pool. When we visited years later, the smallness of this pool amused me. How much bigger things seem when we are young.

My mother, as I said, was a great swimmer. When I was about five, and not yet quite a proficient swimmer and so usually encased in a black inner tube, I managed to up-end myself in that inner tube, my head down and my feet kicking at the clouds. Although she was not the closest to me, (I believe she was outside of the pool compound) upon hearing noise she ran around into the pool area and was the first to reach me and settle me right side up, sputtering and gagging, spitting out pool water with my hair streaming into my eyes and nostrils.

There were other people closer to me, but while they reacted, eyes opened wide with disbelief and mouths shaped in "oh no's", their arms flexed as if to reach out, my mother—with the quick reflexes only a mother possesses, with the built-in antenna that seems to hone in on a child's cry and react like lightning—raced around the fence and reached me first.

An idyll, an Eden, a sweet and golden time—my childhood—my home. But while I had been busy enjoying all of it, my Dad and Mom had been busy working hard to create it. I had a sense of this part of Dad's life but realized that I most likely did not know all of the details. So one day, I flicked on the recorder and asked Dad to tell me all that he remembered about building a home on Arno Road in California, just down the road from where my Mom grew up. My Grandpa Hobday had pioneered that area, and telling the history of the Hobday family would take another book. I knew that there was a road named after him, and I knew that he was one of the earlier settlers in that area. After Mom and Dad were married, he'd made them a very generous gift. I'd heard my dad talk often of how it came about—the first home he had ever owned.

YOUR GRANDPA HOBDAY gave us that 50 acres and we bought the 10 acres for $100 that connected it to the road. I hired T Campbell to help me there; we started digging the foundation by hand, 'cause back then they didn't have no backhoes or nothing and from the first shovel we built that house in 31 days. 'Course I put in long days and your mom put in lots of time doing the finishing work. T Campbell put in time too. It wasn't a fancy house. My brother JT was building the same kind of house at about $10 a square foot. Cost us about $12,000 for that house. We did everything there was—all the drywall and electrical. No inspections were necessary back then. The people who own it now like it and they haven't done nothing to it.

Then I brought a big Cat down and went to work levelling all of the 50 acres and planted it with clover seed; two years made money, then not. I'd work with my brother JT in carpenter work for about eight hours and then come back and work another eight or ten hours. Harold (Helen's brother) was always building something and I'd work for him at night or one of them Van Wormerdams who owned a dairy down the road; often someone wanted me to work with them at night doing something.

I started raisin' those Holstein bull calves and that's what you kids fed up. We had about 50 or 60 there at one time; we'd pick up that dry milk and feed 'em that. You kids would take turns goin' out with the buckets that had a nipple on 'em, and feed those calves through the fence. I'd feed the calves on milk and then turned 'em out in the clover. I'd raise 'em up to about 500 lbs and then sell them as beef, or veal, or they might finish up in the feedlots.

129

I'd raise the clover and get the seed to sell and then raise another crop for pasture. That's why I did the calves. I'd feed those calves to an age and stick them out on that clover pasture and put another 100 pounds on them. It took all that to make a livin'.

When we first went into clover seed it was a dollar a pound; at that time that was a lot of money, but so many people went into it the price dropped quickly—had to borrow from the bank, and when I sold the calves I'd borrow more for the next bunch.

I had to have irrigation so I built a reservoir. All I had to do was to take a carryall (a land mover that gathers land and levels), scrape and dig it out and then put the dirt up above to make a levee which made a natural hole to gather water. Then I had an underground pipe for irrigation. It was about eight foot deep.

You remember those videos of when we drained the reservoir? You must have been about eight years old and you were walking around carrying these big carp. They came in from Deer Creek, through the underground pipe.

I SPENT SOME TIME REMEMBERING. I was sure that if I were to visit that reservoir today, like the house, like Grandpa's pool, it would seem small to me. Only eight foot deep? It had seemed massive then, and my memories float back like the rafts we used to make to dive from and play upon in that reservoir of my childhood.

I remembered riding with Dad on the combine, watching the clover seeds pour into the hopper. I remembered also that we played fort among the hay bales and waded through the reservoir as it drained, catching carp with our bare hands.

We did not eat out, and I know that there were Christmas presents that visited my other friends that I did not receive such as Barbie's Dream House. We did not go to Disney World as some of my other friends did. But I don't remember wanting.

Unfortunately, the high California property taxes combined with a plunge in prices for clover seed and calves meant that we eventually had to sell the 60 acres next to my grandpa Hobday to pay the bills. At this point Dad moved on to the job of his dreams: cattleman.

Thus, our lives irrevocably changed; I was destined to not move on from Arcohe Elementary School to Galt High as did my older brothers and sister, but instead I ended up an 8th grader at Valley Springs Elementary in Northern California and the next year a 9th grader at Baker Middle School in Oregon. Our lives moved on, and our destinies were shaped.

My dad always provided for us. I never went hungry, or shabbily dressed, or slept cold on the ground, or was homeless. But I know that times were not always easy. He and Mom, like all good parents kept this from us, and we lived the active, carefree life that children should live. That's what Dad was raised to do—provide a home for his family, like his father had before him.

Back Roads Of New England

A Song Of Home

Mid pleasures and palaces though we may roam,
Be it ever so humble, there's no place like home.

John Howard Payne

I WAS ONLY SLIGHTLY DISORIENTED when I woke up in my own bed. But the light filtered in through the window, and I recognized my comforter and the soothing sounds of my husband next to me.

I loved traveling, but it was great to get back here. Home. There isn't much else like it. For all that I was raised on the West coast, I have spent the larger portion of my life here in New England.

Certainly a bit of nostalgia accompanied every return I made from the Northwest back to New England, perhaps this year more than ever, because of this journey I had taken with my dad in this second year after my mother's death.

During this time, I had written six songs in six days based on a variety of inspirations, and I wondered now that I was back home, away from a life of leisure spent in airports and pickup trucks, if I could continue to write a song a day? I could, but I had only one more song left in me.

There was some errand that took me from the house today; the errand itself was not important but rather where it led me—to the leafy back roads of New Hampshire. As I drove slowly through a narrow country road, I was drawn to the trees. Perhaps that is because the Western landscape is so different, but it is was if I was seeing them for the first time. It was the height of Summer and the foliage was prominent. Green, leafy skyscrapers surrounded me and, in some places, actually leaned towards each other forming a natural umbrella over the entire road.

The words just started to come:

> There's a canopy above me that I'm driving through
> I can hardly see the clouds that dot the sky of blue.

The tune to the chorus came almost immediately. It tended to build on itself, like a series of waves, and the melody soared. Throughout the day the verses started to come and, by nightfall, the song was finished.

This was the most difficult song of the series and required the most editing. What kind of melody should I put to the verse that complements a chorus that is so soaring? How could I integrate that melody without the song appearing choppy?

The verse melody I come up with was very mild and resided within the confines of a five-note span. The hardest part seemed to be connecting the verse to the chorus. While I had a finished song, I wasn't truly sure if it was performable. Later on, it became obvious to me why this song would not settle in—because the journey was not truly finished. This last song had another role to play.

Back Roads of New England

It seems to me no matter where I roam
I can't escape the siren song of home.
I've stood by the ocean and felt the salty spray.
It seems so wild and free sometimes, I have to turn away
from the menace in its mist and the power in its fist —
the threatening sky of gray.
I've stood in the desert beneath the open sky
and felt so small and naked, the focus of God's eye.
There's something like a prayer that lingers in the air
that's always asking why.
It seems to me no matter where I roam
I can't escape the siren song of home.
Now there's a canopy above me that I'm driving through.
I can hardly see the clouds that dot the skies of blue.
These back roads of New England that I've come home to
seem to soothe the worries of the world.
I've stood in the city and gazed up in the air.
Can't help but admire those concrete canyons everywhere.
But there's just a touch of strife in that jingle-jangle life.
All the rushing here and there.
From the Mississippi Delta to the North Dakota plains
from the Colorado snowcaps to the Carolina rains
it's beautiful and bare, there's clear and frosty air
there's laughter and there's pain.
It seems to me no matter where I roam,
I can't escape the siren song of home.
These back roads of New England that I've come home to
seem to soothe the worries of the world.

Jane Ross Fallon, Summer Acoustic Music Week
Lake Winnipesaukee, New Hampshire, Summer 2010
Photo by Dan Tappan

Twice each summer, musicians descend on a lake in New Hampshire for what has been called "a slice of music heaven." Sponsored by the Boston radio station WUMB, director Dick Pleasants says, "It's an opportunity for you to put aside daily distractions and immerse yourself in folk music, work on your particular skills, and make new friends." The site is beautiful. SAMW is situated on nearly 200 acres of woods and green spaces. With a mile of beach front on Lake Winnipesaukee, SAMW offers a expansive view of the lake and the Ossipee Mountains. For more on SAMW go to www.wumb.org.

PART III

AUGUST 2008

ONE MORE JOURNEY

SIX WEEKS AFTER RETURNING from Oregon, I debuted "Back Roads of New England" at a local music camp called "Summer Acoustic Music Week." For one week we were able to let go of the cares of the world, be fed, and jam all night if we had the stamina.

Touring musicians were invited to give classes in songwriting, guitar, mandolin, fiddle, dulcimer, and much more. There were opportunities to perform as well.

I took a class in songwriting with Cliff Eberhardt, a popular singer/songwriter/guitarist. In this class, he was stressing melody and also the possibility of intros. I had talked with him earlier and we had exchanged our knowledge of the intro as used by some of the Great American Songbook writers such as Cole Porter and Rogers and Hart. I was impressed by his knowledge of the standards.

I thought that this song could use an introduction, and so I added one:

> I've lived in the city, in the sand, and near the water.
> At heart I'm just a simple country farmer's daughter
> and home is where the heart is they say.

I also decided to add an interlude that matched the pace of the intro:

> Life is filled with stress and strife
> and sometimes pain and sorrow—
> left them behind me yesterday,
> they wait for me tomorrow.
> The world is too much with me these days.

At the time, it seemed that the intro and interlude reinforced the nostalgia of home that this song invokes. As I ended my seven day journey, it was home I am thinking of—that sense of place that began this whole adventure. I wanted to reinforce the message that the solace of home can help ease our life's problems.

I sang the song for my roommate, the accomplished musician Sally Sisto, and she loved it. Despite its raggedness, she could hear and appreciate the underlying chord progression of the soaring melody.

"Oh, yes, take that to the class—they will love it," she said.

I waited until Wednesday morning of the week to volunteer to sing it in class—to sing this song, the culmination of my *Seven Songs In Seven Days* journey.

Fate intervened, and on Tuesday night I called Dad out on the West coast. I figured that he was back from my brother Charlie's wedding in Baker City and would want to talk about it. The wedding had been held on the previous Saturday. He had been all set to drive to my brother Daryl's place in Burns and then to drive to the wedding with him and his family.

I heard the receiver lift after a few rings. "Hey Dad, it's Jane," I said.

There was a slight pause. "Oh, hi Jane." His voice sounded weak.

"I just called to see how the wedding was."

Another pause. "Oh, I didn't go to the wedding." His voice was slow and quiet.

Dad's voice, while not overly loud, has always been robust and cheerful. I thought, "Is this my father"?

"You didn't go to the wedding," I said, surprised. "You were really looking forward to it."

"Well, no," he said slowly. He paused. "I had to work for Bagley."

Work for Bagley? Dad would never have promised to work, or let work get in the way of going to this wedding. He was so looking forward to returning to Baker, his many years spent there a fond memory. He was looking forward to seeing his oldest son married and to talking with old acquaintances. My Dad's love of family has grown and blossomed in his waning years. Something did not ring true here.

He seemed distracted. "What are you doing now Dad," I asked.

"Well, I'm trying to get this oxygen machine adjusted. I'm having a little trouble breathing and thought maybe if I could just adjust this thing . . . . " He trailed off.

"Allright, Dad." Silence. "Hey, I'll call you tomorrow to see how it went, OK?"

"OK. Thanks for calling."

As I hung up, I was filled with misgiving. That was not my dad. What sickly, pale ghost had invaded him?

Dad was alone in Bonanza now, with no family nearby. The summer my mother died had brought with it another misfortune—my brother-in-law Bill succumbed to a two-year bout with cancer just four weeks later and my sister Karen, who had lived down the road from Dad, was ready to leave behind the memories and move north, closer to her oldest son and my brothers. She had urged Dad to come with her, but he wasn't ready to leave his home and his friends. I had no nearby family to call.

I had come to SAMW without any of the local numbers of those who watched out for my dad, but I did have my brother Daryl's phone number in the contact list on my cell phone. I called him.

"Daryl, I just got through talking to Daddy. He said he didn't go to the wedding."

"No", said Daryl. "He called and said he had to work for Bagley Friday morning. It was going to be impossible for him to get here by the time we left for Baker."

"Daryl, Dad was really looking forward to this wedding. Didn't you think it odd that he would commit to working for Bagley and let that interfere?"

"Well, yeah, I did a little."

But it hadn't rung any bells for him like it had for me. Perhaps my dad's workaholic past had caught up with him. In his son's mind, it was possible that dad would let the lure of the hayfield, and a commitment to a rancher friend, prevent him from going to his son's wedding. But more likely it is just that he wasn't as tuned in to Dad as I was. My older brother Charlie had called Dad Sunday night, and while he noticed dad was subdued, he didn't think too much of it.

Perhaps it takes a daughter, or perhaps it was because I had spent more time with Dad over the last few years than my brothers had, but I could immediately hear the warning. This was not my dad, and he was in trouble.

"Daryl, I'm really concerned. Dad's not himself." I said. "I don't have numbers for the Northcutts and I can't even remember the last name of Roy and Barbara who live next door. Could you see if you can get hold of someone who can go over and see him?"

After I hung up, I tried calling Dad again and there was no answer, so I left a message. All of my calls after that were not answered. The machine picked up in two rings. Later, I realized that Dad had just not been able to get to the phone in time. My message had put the telephone into ringsaver mode. I called Daryl again.

"I can't get hold of him either, Jane. I tried calling, but he didn't pick up," he told me.

Wednesday morning arrived, and I headed over to my 9 a.m. song writing class, definitely preoccupied. All I could think of was that as soon as the sun came up on the West coast, I was going to call my dad again.

We sat in a circle in the wooden cabin. There were a lot of people there; Cliff's classes were very popular. I decided to go first and get it over with. I sang the song tentatively. It was new and raw, and I still wasn't sure how to integrate the verse with the chorus. When I finished, there was silence. This wasn't unusual. People usually waited until the instructor commented.

Cliff's reaction was swift and honest. "Beautiful melody!" he said, appreciatively. But he wasn't sure about all of the lyrics. "The words in the second verse—I'm listening along to this beautiful song and then suddenly I hear words that are jarring; they make me feel guilty. I don't want to feel guilty, I just want to enjoy the song."

Verse 2 of the first draft went as follows:

I've stood in the city and gazed up in the air.
I can't help but marvel at those concrete canyons there
but I also can't ignore, the homeless and the poor,
they drive me to despair.
And I've been to the suburbs where the houses look the same.
Folks barricade themselves inside;
don't know each other's names.
The money they spend on their houses and their lawns,
it seems like such a shame.

Maybe it was the folksinger in me that always wanted to make a meaningful statement, or maybe it was because I had just spent a lot of time reading about sustainable design when building our new house—I don't know—but this "message" slipped into the song.

Cliff's comments would come back to me eventually, but at the moment I sat there slightly dazed, thinking only that when it was 8 a.m. Pacific time, I was making a phone call.

The class moved on to another student and I picked up my guitar and walked out. I remember the look of surprise on Cliff's face.

Neither he, nor anyone else in the class, knew the stress I was under. My friend, Ken Porter said he followed me out of the class, but I was walking very fast with my head down, so he gave up the chase.

I needed to go somewhere. I needed to clear my head, so I thought I might go into the nearby town of Meredith, New Hampshire and walk around there until I could make that phone call. At the end of the hall on the second floor of the Inn where I was staying was a fire escape. I walked up the four steps to the door and gazed out, thinking I would just go out that way and then head out to my car. But first I thought I should leave a note for Sally.

With much weighing on my mind, I turned quickly, totally forgetting the four steps. One giant stride left me crumpled at the bottom of the stairs, my ankle twisted by the impact.

Luckily, there were people in the adjacent rooms, including a sweet lady named Nancy Eilbert. They rushed for help, and I was soon in my room. The resident nurse felt I should go for x-rays, and the next day was spent lying on my bed recovering with a very badly sprained ankle.

By the time I got to a phone there was no answer. There was no answer at my brother's either. I didn't know what was going on and was in a panic. I spent Thursday night and Friday on crutches or in the prone position, but by Friday night I thought I could perform at the student concert. Urged by sweet Nancy and my roommate, I decided to sing "Back Roads."

"It is a beautiful song," Nancy said. Sally agreed, so I took the plunge.

To take the edge off, I wrote up a humorous introduction about being abducted by songwriter-seeking aliens for the Mistress of Ceremonies, the lovely and gracious performer Lorraine Hammond, to read, and as I was waiting in line for my turn, my cell phone rang.

"I have to take this," I whispered to my friend Duane D'Agnese, who was sitting with me, waiting to help me onto the stage. I hobbled through the lobby and into the office.

"Hi, Jane, it's Daryl. We got Dad to the hospital and he's doing fine. They pumped him full of potassium and he's reviving. Charlie's here too. They are going to keep Dad here for awhile."

Later, Daryl would chastise himself for not jumping into his pickup and heading out to Bonanza immediately. I told him not to beat himself up. It is a four-hour drive from his place, and it was getting late.

He did the right thing by finding someone closer.

The Northcutts, the friends who go to the church my dad went to, live in Malin which is about a 40-minute drive from my dad's. They were the first who came to mind, and Daryl was able to get hold of Les Northcutt. Later I realized that Treude Bagley would have been a closer choice, but it was hard to make decisions quickly.

Les managed to get through to Dad by phone and he agreed that Dad was not himself.

"Jerry would you like me to come over," Les asked.

"Oh, I'm OK. It's getting late." Dad said.

"Well, I'm coming over first thing in the morning."

Les had arrived early the next morning and found dad struggling to put on his jeans. He helped him dress and took him into his doctor in Bonanza who diagnosed dehydration or potassium deficiency. They had called the hospital and immediately put him on an IV.

I was flooded with relief but not free from worry. I had an overwhelming desire to be there, to be with him, to see for myself that he was well.

It was my turn to take the stage, and I won't relive the details too explicitly. It was perhaps the worse performance of my life. I tell my Public Speaking students that one way to beat stage fright is to eliminate as many unknowns as possible and to practice—if the unknown surfaces, muscle memory will then kick in. Well, singing a brand new, loosely polished song in a stressful situation is not a good choice.

I remember feeling uncertain as I sang; it was all in slow motion. Each word was a chore to get out, and I was very relieved when my time on stage was over.

As I headed for the exit, Ken Porter came after me. He had seen me perform before and he knew I was capable of better. "It's OK. This is SAMW. It's a beautiful song." Another friend, Claude Galinski, rushed over from where he was doing sound and just looked at me, stunned.

I quickly left the building and hobbled to the Inn where I had left my things packed up and ready to go. A fellow camper who had been helping with sound, Don Travins, followed me to the Inn and handed me the CD of my performance with a bemused look on his face.

I managed to pull my car up in front of the Inn and load it up. Several friends gathered round to wish me well. "Are you sure you are ready to drive?" someone asked.

"It's an automatic with cruise control," I said. "I'll be fine." So I managed the two-hour drive home.

I called my husband and told him to expect me around 10 p.m. and spent Saturday resting and getting ready. On Sunday morning, I left my crutches behind me, donned my air cast, and headed out from Boston to Klamath Falls. I never did listen to that concert CD.

For months previous, Dad had been waking with headaches. His doctor had felt unsettled by this, saying that he had never known morning headaches to be anything but a problem. He was mostly concerned by the possibility of an aneurysm. The specialist that Norma Northcutt had recommended had felt that same way. They had wanted Dad to go in for an MRI, but Dad couldn't handle being cramped up in the machine given his body's aches and pains, so he never did it. In the end, perhaps a CT scan would have been a better choice because the real problem was slow bleeding. My dad was having a long, drawn out "wet" stroke.

The thought of him alone for days, fumbling with his oxygen, with no one around just broke my heart. He hadn't had to work for Bagley. He was embarrassed to tell Daryl that he had wrecked both his car and his pickup. In fact, he had inadvertently cut himself off from the folks in the area who look out for him. Because there was no car in the driveway, Treude Bagley assumed he had gone to the wedding in it. And, because he knew about the wedding, Paul Northcutt had not called when Dad missed church that Sunday. Events had conspired to leave him alone at this particular time.

Dad remembers those days with a sense of disbelief. "I knew what I was doing but had no control over it," he said. Scheduled to visit the optometrist, he ended up going at the wrong time of day. He went at night.

"I went to the eye people," he had told me on the phone. "But when I got there, they were closed. It was really dark by the time I got home."

"Dark, Dad? They aren't open at night. What were you doing driving around in the dark?"

What he didn't tell me was that on the way home, he'd shot right past his driveway. When he'd realized this, he'd made a u-turn without de-accelerating and in the process had taken down a neighbor's fence.

His car was in tough shape, so the next morning he'd taken it to the local auto repair and left it.

Meanwhile, he'd driven his pickup to see his doctor during his office hours in Bonanza. The doctor sent him into town (Klamath Falls, about 45 minutes away) for medication. While pulling out of the office, he'd been hit by another car, which severely dented his vehicle.

On the way to town, he'd become disoriented and somehow ended up in the mountains outside of the city. As he'd slowly climbed over the desolate, windy mountain roads, his pickup came to a halt. The battery, jarred considerably, had become disconnected.

It was night. As he had sat there in the pickup, he knew he didn't have the strength to even open the hood. A couple of high school girls came by and asked if he needed help, and he was not sure why, but he said that no, that he was OK.

Well, he had sat there all night in that pickup, on that lonely mountain road. Morning came and somehow he'd been able to prop up the hood with the help of a branch that he'd found on the side of the road and reseat the battery. He'd made it to the next town just as his gas gauge was reading empty where he'd filled up before going home.

He told me of these adventures only after the fact; he knew I wouldn't much like them.

My son, Patrick, has said, "Your dad's a horse." A hearty soul for sure. I had read once that Ross is the German nickname for someone who resembled a horse. So maybe he is.

I SAT IN MY DAD'S KITCHEN one more time. He was happy to be home. I had arrived at the hospital in Klamath Falls on Sunday afternoon, rented a car and headed straight in from the airport. My brothers, Charlie and Daryl, were in the hospital room with my Dad. He was propped up, looking wan but well, with an IV hooked up.

I hugged him, and we chatted about his condition and relived a little bit the circumstances that had led him there.

"Hello, Mr. Ross," the nurse said cheerily, as she arrived in the room to take his blood pressure and to write what it was she needed to write on her pad.

"When can I get out of here?" Dad said. He was itching to put on some real clothes and looked very uncomfortable in his hospital johnny.

"Well, Mr. Ross, your vital signs are very good and given this family support, I'd say we can probably discharge you today."

Dad wasted no time getting into his jeans and cowboy shirt. Hospital life was not for him.

The boys went back to their respective homes; they both had long drives. I settled in to take care of Dad until he got back on his feet. My ankle was still bothering me; I knew I had thrown the crutches away prematurely, but I hadn't wanted the encumbrance of them on the plane. I could take care of the ankle when I got back home.

Dad leaned against the kitchen peninsula, his face pale.

"I can drive," he said.

"Daddy," I said, "I know you can drive, but you need to give it some time. Make sure that you're strong, as much for you as for the other drivers on the road."

He looked woebegone, and I knew that the ability to drive is a part of his self-esteem. He had always been able to drive and always exercised his patriarchal right to do so.

"Remember Mom, Dad? Remember how she stopped driving when she felt the Parkinson's medication was making her sleepy? She didn't want to risk hurting someone else. It was a tough decision for her to make. You will drive again but wait awhile; wait until you're healthy."

That night my brother Ernie called.

"I've been up all night," he said. "Karen and I didn't come to the hospital because it's a six-hour drive, and we knew that Charlie, and Daryl, and you, would be there. I figured I should just stay here until I found out what it was that was needed of me.

"I've been making a list and it is obvious that Dad needs to come here. I have everything he needs. I have the horses and the barn, and I can put up a mobile on my property, and no one is going to bother me about it."

My heart filled with warmth and appreciation for Ernie. He'd never married and had never had children. His life had been basically just taking care of himself. At an early age, he'd realized that he needed to be his own boss, and so he'd focused on horseshoeing as a career and gone to Arizona to learn the trade.

Previously, he had bought himself 20 acres of land on an undeveloped road near Goldendale, WA. He'd paid for it in cash and developed it slowly. In fact, I think he was the first resident on a road that is now populated with many homes; there is even a side road named after him. Buying only what he could pay for with cash, he'd built his cabin, his barn, and lived without running water, plumbing, or TV for years.

And so, knowing the fear that might strike at the heart of a bachelor upon accepting the challenge of caring for an elderly parent, I was more than appreciative of Ernie's offering.

"Karen has said she will put up the money for a Single Wide for Dad. We found what we think is a good one. It has a bump out, so that will give him more room and, unlike some, it has a full size shower. We can park it next to my cabin. He can have his independence but I will be able to check in on him every day."

My heart gave a great big sigh of relief. Thank you Ernie.

"You know, Ern," I reassured him, "Dad is healthy. He will be able to look after himself. And if there comes a time when he needs more, then the rest of us will help you with that."

And so, Ernie worked hard to get the place ready for Dad so that he could settle in before the depth of winter. Daddy was moved over to Goldendale, Washington by November.

When Mom died, I had spent a great deal of time cleaning and so there wasn't as much to do as there might have been to get Dad ready to leave. The majority of the furniture we left. That would have to be stored. All dad would be able to fit into his new home would be his TV, his easy chair, his computer stand, and his bed. The dining room table, the couch, the second bed, and extra chairs—none would fit into the new space.

I had to get back to the East Coast, but when I left I knew that Dad would be OK. They had solved his hemorrhage with a massive transfusion of potassium and an admonition to get off the aspirin he had been inhaling in an attempt to relieve his body's aches. He was lucid and able to drive.

The first thing Dad did when we got back to his place from the hospital was fix his pickup. The battery that had stranded him on the mountain pass was still loose. He was very weak and lacked the strength to reseat the battery himself. And so, he stood at my elbow as we propped up the pickup's hood and went to work. As he guided me, I tightened the bolts that held the battery in place. Then I put a hand under his arm and steadied him and walked him back to his chair.

I could imagine the relief he felt; his truck was now operational. It would be there for him when he was ready.

And so, Gerald Dwane Ross made another journey, one of many he had made in his life. Reluctant to leave his home, but shaken by the blood hemorrhage that had left him incapable of making lucid decisions, he packed up and moved, grateful for the love of his children and ready to deal with whatever this new life might bring. When I went out to visit him at Christmas, I found him settled in—a bit cramped but with everything he might need.

Honor your parents. Perhaps we are not so far removed from that generation, the generation that hung together. My dad gave his earnings to his parents so that they could buy a house and own a dairy. He gave it with no thought for his own needs; it was what was expected of him and what he wanted to do. And now it had come full circle, and my brother Ernie would fulfill his obligation, his filial love, and watch over the man who had worked long hours to see that he had a roof over his head and food on the table— the man who raised him.

AFTERWARD

"Bagley called," Dad says, "and he was saying he sure wished that I'd come down and help him with the hayin'; he said that I could cut more hay than four or five of them others. Says I can cut more hay accidentally then others do on purpose."

I smile. "Daddy, you can't do that."

"It's just sittin' around in an air-conditioned cab," he protests.

"Right. Until the engine dies and you try to crawl under it to fix it, and when you can't you walk the mile back to the house. No Dad. You can't do that anymore."

He laughs. "Well, in my mind, I can do anything."

It has been almost three years since Dad left his home in Bonanza, Oregon, and gone to live with my brother. Little by little, they have worked to make his hasty residence a home. This summer commences an addition on to the side of his home that will allow for some expansion.

"I'll have some room for a nice fold-out sofa for you to sleep on when you come," he tells me. "You won't have to sleep on the camp cot."

But we manage. I have visited him here twice a year since his stroke and we have taken a couple of more journeys together and plan to take more. My Dad, who never cooked except for over an open fire when my mom was healthy, has become quite the gourmet, hunting for recipes on the internet and buying exotic spices. He often cooks extra and gives some to Ernie when he comes home late from shoeing horses somewhere.

He is a gracious host and likes to show off his prowess when I arrive, however, he doesn't mind having some help in the kitchen either, and we manage to share the small space as we put the evening meal together.

My dad is a carnivore. Maybe it was all of those cornbread meals he ate as a kid. I steam the broccoli and boil and mash the potatoes, as he carefully seasons the rib eye with something called "Montreal Steak Rub" and forks it into the large George Foreman grill that my brother Daryl gave him for Christmas.

"Makes it almost as good as grillin'," Dad says. "Helps on the days when I can't go out and use the grill on the porch."

After 10 minutes, he turns the steaks and resets the lid. When they are done he transfers them to our plates.

It is evening. My Arkansas traveler is tired; he has come a long way from a sharecropper's cabin in Arkansas to the Sacramento Valley, and into the deserts of Oregon. He settles wearily into his seat at the dining room table.

"Um," he said, digging in. "Pretty good. Wonder what the poor people eat?"

I glanced around his modest Single Wide abode, at the worn carpet that needs to be replaced, and smile. Indeed. What do the poor people eat?

Jerry Ross and Ernie Ross, August 2010
Back in the saddle.

PART IV

THE EDITING PROCESS

AN IMPORTANT PART OF SONGWRITING is editing. I am amazed at how completely I was able to develop each song within a day's time; however, I couldn't just leave them in their first form. Good writing is good editing, so when I had finished this series of songs, I began taking them to my songwriting group for feedback. I incorporated some of the suggested changes and decided to ignore others. That is what editing is about. Is editing cheating? Didn't I commit to writing a song a day?

Well, I did write the songs, and I did commit them to my digital recorder. There you have it: seven songs, completed in seven days. (The song lyrics that are included in this text at the end of each chapter are the final lyrics, and they contain the changes that were made after the first version was written.)

However, while complete, the original songs were not be the best they could be and to test them I needed to try them out on an audience. Just because a song is ostensibly complete, it doesn't mean it is a good song; I want good songs. It would be pretty easy to write seven bad or mediocre songs!

Helping me out was a mostly constant, but sometimes shifting, cast of characters, songwriters themselves: Ellen Schmidt, Terence Hegarty, Mary Pratt, Steve Rapson, Chris Gerstner, Deborah Rocha, Suzanne Owens, Jon McAuliffe, Jon Waterman, Dawn Frost, Alex Solomonoff, John Schindler, and Betsy Binstock.

THE CAST OF CHARACTERS

Ellen Schmidt (hostess): Ellen is a fine singer-songwriter and has recorded two CDs of original music. "When I perform," says Schmidt, "I want to communicate with everyone in the room so they feel energized and uplifted. I want my songs to help people find the best in themselves." She does. See www.ellenschmidt.com for more about Ellen and her music.

Steve Rapson: Steve is an excellent guitarist who is well known among the Boston area folk community and beyond. Not only a solo performer who has produced seven CDs of his own performance, he has also collaborated on several others. Additionally he is a performance coach and has authored the best-selling book, *The Art of the Solo Performer*. Go to www.sologuitar.com for more about Steve.

Jon Waterman: Singer and songwriter Jon Waterman writes and performs the roots-driven blend of classic country, blues, and roots rock that is currently classified as Americana. His 2010 CD received praise from critics and was rated as one of the top ten New England CD releases of 2010 in The Noise Magazine. Read about Jon at www.jonwaterman.com.

Betsy Binstock: Performance poet and writer of fine songs, Betsy is a member of the Folksong Society of Greater Boston and the author of several books of poetry. Her poetic sense is always most appreciated.

Deborah Rocha: A talented singer-songwriter who specializes in the vibrant sounds of Brazil, Deborah has collaborated with Steve Rapson on a CD called "Breeze." More about Deborah at www.myspace.com/Deborahrocha.

Terence Hegarty: A staple on the folk-music scene, Terence is known for his literate lyrics and imaginative guitar arrangements. He has produced a CD of original music with Steve Rapson. Visit Terence at www.myspace.com/ terencehegarty.

Jon McAuliffe: Involved in music since his very early years, Jon has been part of many bands and was once a staff writer for United Artists. He has just released his first solo CD, "In This Present Form." Jon's website is www.jonmcauliffe.com.

Suzanne Owens: A graduate of the American Musical and Dramatic Academy in New York City, she attended the Guildhall of Music and Drama London England and has won many awards for her books of poetry, and has been published in many journals. Suzanne is not a songwriter but a wordsmith of the highest order whose critiques are always valued.

<u>Mary Pratt</u>: Mary often supports and is supported by Terence Hegarty. She is folk-acoustic singer-songwriter from Holliston, Massachusetts, whose background includes many years performing as a soprano and soloist in the Hancock Church choir in Lexington and Alan Lanom's Mystic Chorale.

<u>Alex Solomonoff</u>: Alex attends the songwriting group sporadically, but when he comes he always engages everyone with his songs and his apt commentary. Find him at www.myspace.com/alexsolomonoff.com.

<u>Chris Gerstner</u>: A Needham, MA resident Chris is known for her fine singing voice and well-written compositions. She recently released a CD of original music, "My Own Little Heaven," produced by Steve Rapson in 2010. Read more at www.myspace.com/chrisgerstner.com.

<u>John Schindler</u>: This award-winning songwriter, known for his insightful songs of ordinary life, comes to the group occasionally, and I was fortunate to have him there to hear one or two of these songs. Visit John at www.johnschindler.net.

Note:

These are the songwriting group members who happened to be present when I was editing these songs. There are many more who attend and have helped me greatly on other songs, such as Richard Eilbert, Mark Stepakoff, Carolyn Waters, Laura Gold, and Cheryl Perreault, among others.

SONG ONE

IT'S COLD OUTSIDE

A group of people milled around in the kitchen when I arrived at 12:30 that Sunday afternoon. They were making sandwiches and chatting informally. This is how the sessions begin. At 1 p.m., the songs begin to be shared and commented on. Often the participants choose to write comments on the lyric sheets that are passed out.

Ellen Schmidt is sometimes called the godmother of the open mikes in the greater Boston area. In her 70's, she astounds all with her energy and devotion to the musical arts. Once a month, she holds a songwriting critique at her house in Concord, Massachusetts. Usually there are between 10 and 20 folks there, playing their new songs and inviting feedback from each other.

Today I shared "It's Cold Outside," and as I passed out the lyric sheets, I explained the history of my exercise. I finished singing the song and tried to get the feel for the response from the expressions of those in the circle. I felt a basically positive response and opened it up to comments.

The first comment was from Deb Rocha. "It seems that singing "It's cold outside" twice is too repetitive. I think it would help to not have the repeat. It seems unnecessary and doesn't add anything to the song." I agreed and removed the repeat.

Jon Waterman had remained pretty quiet throughout the discussion but had one comment: "I like the chorus." Well, that's enough for me—the chorus stays.

Alex quietly spoke up. "Maybe there should be a reason that the speaker devises to go visit the old friend. Perhaps he or she could be returning the scarf, for instance?"

Hmm. The second verse as penned read "Maybe I'll try out that new scarf to protect me against the wind." Yes, take back a borrowed scarf—great excuse. Good idea. I included it.

Somebody asked about the personal connection. Ah yes, the personal connection.

THE PERSONAL CONNECTION

The well-known folksinger and songwriter Bob Franke is known for his songwriting courses, and he is famous for declaring that all songs are fiction. He says, "Treating songs as fiction gives students both privacy and the freedom to borrow from their own lives. All my songs are fiction, even if sometimes they look like docudrama. When I sing my song I am both actor and playwright. My goal is not to expose my life but to find truths that I share with my audience, and to articulate them in a useful way."

Audiences are often determined to find the personal connection. Someone once wrote me after a performance that he was, "mesmerized by the beauty of your lyrics and intrigued as to where they might have come from—what personal experiences do you draw from?"

"Write what you know" is the basic premise of creative writing courses—but how often do we just get tired of some people who write song after song of autobiography that leaves us longing for a good old rock and roll tune. Confessional songwriting, [cynics have been known to dub it "navel gazing"] probably emerged most noticeably on the singer-songwriter scene with Joni Mitchell's *Blue* album, and the music world is littered with many others who drew almost exclusively from personal feelings and events to craft their work.

Somehow, in songwriting more than novels, we expect this personal connection, even though there are many autobiographical novelists as well. I think that this is because the genre (songwriting) usually includes a performance aspect—because we are the ones singing the words, and because we want to make the song believable and from the heart, we must put ourselves into it. The audience, then, assumes that each word that escapes our lips is the unadulterated, unvarnished truth.

In the case of "It's Cold Outside," the lyrics wrote themselves so fast that I was not reflecting on any similar personal relationship. In this case, I won't even worry about what the audience might think. The song reflects upon the type of experience everyone has had, in some form or another. Words are often hard to muster, failing friendships difficult to ignite, and people are stubborn about saying" I'm sorry." This song is possible only in the first person and works best that way.

SONG TWO

BLUE DRESS

I wasn't sure how the group would react to this song; it seemed so simple and homespun. I wasn't sure they would relate.

Most songs need several edits before being through, but this one seemed almost perfect from the beginning.

Everyone seemed to like the song. Betsy Binstock wrote on her lyric sheet that I might want to change "trying hard to please" to "a photo meant to please." I gave that serious thought. Certainly that would be a big clue to the audience what was going on. But it seemed to me that what I meant to convey was the overall demeanor of my mother—not in just this particular instance. So, I kept the original lyric.

Steve Rapson proclaimed it a lovely song and Suzanne Owens felt that the story line was strong and compelling. I looked around. Terence? He smiled. Mary? She nodded. So I guess this song was good to go. There were very few suggestions for this song. Sometimes a song comes quite easily and completely. That was the case with this song.

SONG THREE

LONG AND LONELY NIGHT

The song was generally well received by the songwriting group. They found it beautiful and moving. There were a few small word changes suggested. For instance, I had referred to a lone mountain on the landscape as a "solo" sentinel and Terence suggested "sole" and I realized that the word "solo" has a performance connotation. It is usually used in conjunction with an activity, whereas, "sole" definitely means alone. I liked the feeling of a two-syllable word there, however, and ended up going with "silent" sentinel. Several people commented on the strength of the last line, "and I wonder if I'll see you there throughout my long and lonely life."

Jon Waterman did bring up the conundrum—the speaker has not yet lived her entire life—can she assume it will be long and lonely? The general consensus was that the line was strong because of the other mentions of "long and lonely" and that it made sense for the protagonist to wonder in a moment of quiet solitude if her life would be that way forever.

Chris Gerstner wrote that she particularly liked the way that phrase "long and lonely" was used throughout the song in different ways. She also brought up another word issue: she felt the word "starkness" might be mistaken for darkness. I gave that some thought and knew that this was a potential problem. But I liked the word "starkness" so much, that I kept it.

There were a couple of comments about whether the "you" was the same "you" throughout, but most people seemed to think so. A couple of people felt that the time tag in the last verse was confusing but again I chose to leave it because I felt that the audience would get it.

"Long and Lonely seems like an easy way out with the title," Mary pointed out.

"Any other ideas?" I asked." How about "The Old Cowgirl's Lament?" Jon McAuliffe, who felt the song was strong, latched on to this one. "Whoo! That's a great title" he laughs. But, I couldn't bring myself to use it. So, in general, I found very few things to change in this song, written in a few hours while Dad and drove through the desert.

SONG FOUR

CATHERINE NEWMAN DUNCAN

I sang this a cappella to the songwriting group, and the basic response was positive.

The song just sprang from what I knew of the migration traditions of the late 19th century. The form again is a narrative, even more so than

Blue Dress, which has a more modern structure including verses and a chorus. "Catherine Newman Duncan" is more along the lines of the Child ballads like "Sir Patrick Spens" or "Barbara Allen." It reminds me a little of "The Gypsie Laddie" in content (where the daughter of the house takes off with the gypsy, forsaking the luxuries of her upbringing.) There is no form except for the repetition of the verses that are telling the story. It isn't strict ballad form, however, and contains an uneven "bridge" arrangement. There are two couplets in a different melody and tempo after the fourth stanza. These are followed by two stanzas, and then two more couplets, then the songs ends with a stanza. Since this format didn't bother anyone, I wasn't concerned. As many a folk musician has told me, irregularities aren't issues as long as you play things the same way all the time.

In fact, there was very little that they suggested changing. Someone insisted that the song be sung only a cappella. We discussed briefly whether or not a rhythm instrument, especially an old fashioned one like spoons would be good. One general comment was that it could go a little slower. I took these comments into consideration and they are reflected in the final performance of the song.

Jon Waterman was concerned that Willie didn't ask Catherine to marry him until they were already on their way. To me, though, that aspect says a lot about Catherine—a woman willing to defy convention.

I changed some words from the initial version:

S1/ "She means the world to me" became "she's all the world to me," and "But Kate said don't you listen to him" became "But she held tight and said don't listen."

S2/ Jon Waterman pointed out the similarity of "they ran through the brambles and they ran through the bushes" to the phrase in the folk song, "The Battle of New Orleans"; in fact, it is the same phrase. So I changed it to "they ran up the hills and they ran down the valleys." It is fresher that way.

[Jon did make me wonder how much this song owes to this old Jimmy Driftwood song. It has a similar cadence and also mentions travel—"down the Mississippi to the Gulf of Mexico." My family liked to pen the occasional parody and I remember my brothers and sister and I sang a version of this when were in the mountains with Lombardis:

> In 1966 we took a little trip
> Along with Colonel Curly (Lombardi)
> Down the mighty Silver Crick.
> We took a little beans and a little caviar
> And we took a great big bucket of big cigars.

That's how we entertained ourselves in a cabin in the woods with no television.]

I had already changed "they fought tornados, suffered blizzards, survived torrential rains," to "they fought injuns and wildfires, and suffered torrential rains" but Jon Waterman felt that "injuns" might not be politically correct. It probably wasn't but it seemed to fit the time period. I changed it to "they fought outlaws," which is just as good.

Another major lyrical change came in the second bridge: "Times were hard but she was tough and stood the wind and drought and became a local legend before her light went out," became "Life was hard but she put up a fight and became a living legend before death put out her light."

Finally the last stanza changed quite a bit on the side of conciseness.

The original was:

> They took her to a quiet place just outside of town
> and in the cold of February they laid her body down.
> Oh what do you dream of Catherine Newman Duncan
> when you hear the pine trees moan.
> Do you wish that you were sleeping in feathers
> in your old Kentucky home.

This, of course, is a bit ragged and I replaced it with:

> They took her down to the outskirts of town
> and in a February thaw they laid her body down.
> Oh what do dream of Catherine Newman Duncan
> when you hear the North wind moan?
> Are you glad that you left your feather bed
> in your old Kentucky home?

Lyrical differences like this occur sometimes as I sing a song to myself over and over, and whatever lyrics seem best suited to the song will replace the original ones. Other than that, the song got a thumb's up from the writer's group.

SONG FIVE

CHURCH PEOPLE

I was a little uncertain as to how "Church People" was going to be received by the songwriting group. Would the religious theme turn anyone off, I wondered? How many would empathize with the small-town church experience?

Several people felt that I should not start with the chorus. Other than that, the suggestions were limited to word choice.

"You really capture the flavor," wrote Ellen, and Steve called it a "fine song." They each had comments about certain phrases that seemed stilted. Ellen felt that "black patent leather shoes and white socks for me" was awkward. Yes, it was a mouthful! But those old patent leather Mary Janes are a part of my memory of what it meant to be dressed up as a little girl. I changed it to "little white socks and shiny shoes" and that made it easier to sing.

Steve felt that "church people helped him keep his heart, his health, his home" seemed a little clinical. That became "helped him heal is heart, and keep his home." Jon Waterman also observed that "disaster, death, and sorrow" seemed excessively dramatic, so I changed it to "when the sorrows of this world."

Someone else wrote (and I am not certain who this was) that the phrase "There's nothing that will lift you up like God's community," was a little jarring. I changed this to "There's nothing that will lift you like that love so full and free."

Other than some word shifting and some advice to slow the tempo, "Church People" got the thumbs up. Ellen came up to me afterward and said how she particularly liked the detail such as the mention of the beautiful hymn, "Precious Memories."

When we were preparing to record this my bass player, Steve Gilligan, came up with another suggestion. He didn't like the chorus between the first and second verses because it interrupted the flow. The first verse ends with my mother, and the second verse begins with her.

Taking out the choruses made it a fairly short song, but repeating the chorus at the end lengthened it, and emphasizing the chorus was appropriate given its importance in the song.

SONG SIX

SHORT ENDINGS TO LONG GOODBYES

I chose to play this song on the piano, and I know that singing the song to myself in the car before I was able to sit down and work out chords on the piano allowed me to make changes without realizing it.

The melody changed some from the original, as did some of the words.

The response on the part of the songwriting group was positive for this song as it had been for the others. Jon W. focused on two sentences that he felt were awkward:

> They're entwined so tightly, could not get a thing between" and
> "A distant, disembodied voice …

And so I changed them to:

> to separate the two of them would take extraordinary means" and
> "I hear a distant voice.

The first version had a complete chorus at the beginning and between each verse. Steve Rapson felt that there were too many choruses, and so I scaled the first down to an intro line and removed all but one chorus, substituting a musical intro for the other. Other than that, there was general approval of the song.

Later, Steve Gilligan made a major structural change as we prepared to record the song. He suggested starting right with the story and forgetting the intro. He also felt that the chorus was very strong and needed more repetition. So instead of ending directly with the key phrase (wet tears on fresh young faces, short endings to long good-byes), he suggested singing the chorus one more time and then using the previous phrase as a coda. I liked this approach and so performed the song that way.

This song gets a strong response from people. They feel the story is very visual and very timely given our current military situation in Iraq and Afghanistan. This is a scene being played out across America in airports everywhere.

SONG SEVEN

BACK ROADS OF NEW ENGLAND

The comment I had received from Cliff Eberhardt came back to me. His reaction had been immediate and honest. That kind of reaction, coming from an accomplished songwriter, is worth paying attention to. I had a chance to see him in performance at a house concert sometime later, and I was touched that the first thing he said was, "How's your dad," and gave me a big hug.

I didn't have a chance to tell him that I had taken his advice. In revising this song, I took out the preachy-ness. He was right. It didn't fit. The new verse two had no accusations, no guilt, nothing to detract from the beauty of the melody and the nostalgia it creates.

I sang the song out at open mikes a few times, little by little getting used to the verse meeting the chorus, and felt that the change from verse to chorus was a problem that could be solved through performance.

By the time I took the song to songwriting group, I had removed the awkward passages, the intro, and the interlude. Instead, I had written a new beginning line:

> It seems to me no matter where I roam,
> I cannot escape the siren song of home.

This line caught the attention of John Schindler. It was a line he especially liked. So I not only left it in, I sang it again at the end of each verse. This touch, I felt, really helped the verse to transition melodically into the chorus.

Besides this, I made few changes. I replaced the "suburbs" section with a tribute to other geographical landscapes throughout our great country. Steve Rapson felt that this wasn't necessary. He felt it was fine to go right to the chorus from the end of the first half of verse two. I could see his point—but I liked to keep the song balanced so I left it in.

In retrospect, I realized that the verse was reminiscent of a line in "Catherine Newman Duncan":

> From the Mississippi Delta to the North Dakota plains,
> they fought outlaws and wild fires and suffered torrential rains.

I notice now that in the draft at my side, I have written "North Dakota badlands to the cold Nebraska plains, from the Colorado snowcaps to those Carolina rains" but when I sang the song in performance I found that I had gone back to "Mississippi Delta and North Dakota Plains."

I think that's OK. In fact, it makes this series of songs even more connected—like a song cycle with the ending harkening back to something in the middle. I like it. It's good to be back.

PART V

THE RECORDING

SEVEN SONGS IN SEVEN DAYS

TRACK LIST

Welcome by G.S. Picard (0:24)
The Seven Songs:
1. It's Cold Outside (1:51)
2. Blue Dress (3:09)
3. Long and Lonely Night (3:46)
4. Catherine Newman Duncan (3:12)
5. Church People (2:20)
6. Short Endings to Long Goodbyes (3:55)
7. Back Road of New England (3:50)

EXTRAS:
Come Journey With Me (2:11)
She Appeared to Be 18 or 19 Years Old (1:51)
sung by Jerry Ross (Traditional)

Jane Fallon: Vocals, keyboard on "Come Journey".
Jeff Root: Rhythm guitar.
Steve Gilligan: Electric bass guitar, harmony on
"It's Cold Outside".
Rob Carlson: Lead Guitar on "It's Cold Outside",
Dobro on all other tracks.
Bob Francis: Mandolin
Tom Ruckey: Percussion
Tag Vennard: Keyboard on "Short Endings" and "Long and
Lonely Night"; Washboard on "Catherine Newman Duncan"
Jon Swenson: Harmony, "Church People"
Jerry Ross: Vocals, "She Appeared To Be 18 or 19 Years Old"

CD Mixed and Mastered by Jeff Root at The Root Cellar, Westminster, Massachusetts.

© 2011, Jane Fallon, all rights reserved.

All songs by Jane Fallon except for "She Appeared To Be 18 or 19 Years Old." (Traditional)

THE BAND

Jeff Root (Producer, Guitar)

A software engineer by trade, Jeff has been active at various levels in the Boston music scene since 1978, performing with acts as varied as Leon Redbone, J. Geils, and Edgar Winter. He has recorded 14 CD's both solo and with collaborators during the course of his career. The great producer of Beatles' fame, George Martin, proclaimed Jeff's 1974 recording Idiot's Delight, "the best home-grown recording I've ever heard." In 1980, his song "Tune Into Me" was the #1 song in Boston for eight weeks and his most recent CD received generous airplay as well. Jeff's production talents equal his composition and performing skills He is gaining a stellar reputation in his "Root Cellar Studio" where he is is in high demand. Jeff played on Jane Fallon's Gemini Rising CD, mixing and co-producing four tunes and creating the final master. Without his help, the live recording of "Seven Songs in Seven Days"would never had happened. For more information see www.jeffroot.com

Stephen Gilligan (Bass player, Co-production, Harmony)

After leaving Berklee College of Music in Boston in 1976, Steve spent a year with The Open Road Band, a folk rock quartet out of western Massachusetts. He moved back to Boston in the Fall of 1977 and became a charter member of Boardwalk and Mercury recording artist The Stompers, one of New England's most popular rock 'n' roll bands during the '80s and into the '90s. Acoustic music was always in his heart, and in 1997 he formed the acoustic trio City of Roses. During their 12 years together, City of Roses recorded two critically acclaimed CDs and shared the stage with Jane Fallon numerous times. Steve found a kinship in Jane's music and joined Jane for her performance at the Boston Folk Festival in 2007. He has performed on Jane's *City Girl* and *Gemini Rising* CDs. In addition to his work with Jane, he continues to write and perform original roots Americana music as a member of the Jon Macey and Steve Gilligan duo, and with the seminal Boston rock band Fox Pass. www.foxpassmusic.com

Thomas Ruckey (Drums)

Tom is an amazing drummer, a professional musician, and an electrical engineer who teaches drums and has also arranged and taught drum lines and marimba. He is also a talented bass player and has appeared on many Root Cellar CDs by Jeff Root, Gayle Picard, Lee Villaire, Karl Sharicz, and others.

Robert Carlson (Dobro and Guitar)

Rob graduated from Berklee College in 1997. He focused on jazz arranging, the music of Brazil, and lyric writing and since then has been hard at work as a songwriter and performer. He has opened for the following artists: Johnny Winter, Edgar Winter, Ronnie Earl, Roomful of Blues, James Cotton, Sugar Blue (Rolling Stones Harmonica player), Vassar Clements, Treat Her Right, Matt "Guitar" Murphy (Blues Brothers), Luther Johnson, Moses Roscoe, and Jimmy Buffet at the Tweeter Center (Bud Tent). He received two Billboard Certificate Awards for two of his songs on a blues rock CD. One tune got to number six on the UK Demo Chart 1991. Rob wrote six tunes for the Caribbean/reggae band Dell Smart and Exit/In's latest CD: "Sure 'YA Right!". Ronnie Earl and Paul Rishell are featured on separate tracks. This CD has received airplay in Belize City, St.Thomas/Virgin Islands, LA, MD and NYC and received good recognition from a performance on FOX TV 10. Rob also contributed lyrics and music to a score by Zeca Barros for a Brazilian indie film "Frontiera." Rob and his partner in Brazil, Guilherme Vaz, have started a production company called RWCSagaz. They're getting a lot of local musicians to record, which contributes to a variety of musical styles. For more on Rob go to www.myspace.com/robcarlson.

Bob Frances (Mandolin)

From psychedelic guitar rock to Celtic melodies on Irish Bouzouki, Bob moves from instrument to instrument and genre to genre with the ease of a seasoned player. Bob has been an area musician since the late 60's and has played and recorded in a number of Rock, Folk and Celtic groups. These days he is very active in the "open mic" scene, adding a bit of humor with his own songs and an "edgy twist" to his cover songs. Bob is also a highly sought after studio musician. His tasteful licks, on guitar, mandolin and bouzouki, can be heard on the CD's, of many New England artists.

<u>Tag Vennard</u> (Keyboard, Washboard)

Tag was raised in Westford Mass, where he taught himself the piano and guitar. He has been playing these since his teenage years, stopping only long enough to raise two beautiful children. He is happily married to Karen Anne Vennard and lives in Salem NH. He can be seen at the local open mics, sometimes at the Java Room in Chelmsford and on Facebook. Tag enjoys all forms of art. Besides being a musician he is a Sunday painter and some of his work can be seen at the Gallery At Floral Arts on Rte.110 in Westford, Massachusetts.

THE RECORDING

Seven Songs In Seven Days was recorded live at The Bull Run Restaurant (www.bullrunrestaurant.com) in Shirley, Massachusetts, on Oct. 14th, 2010. I can't thank enough the brilliant musicians who pulled this off in one take with only one practice.

I also want to thank the tremendous audience of friends, family, and fans who came out that night to support this endeavor, with a special thanks to Gayle Picard, whose industriousness and belief in the power of the independent singer-songwriter created this special opportunity.

In addition, I extend my very special thanks to the songwriters who shared the stage with me during the second half of that very special night:

Jon Swenson
Tom Smith (www.tomsmithmusic.com)
Mark Stepakoff (www.markstepakoff.com)
Jon McAuliffe (www.jonmcauliffe.com)

I am privileged to know many immensely talented songwriters and sharing the evening with these four musicians, and singing some of their songs, was a special treat for me.

The combined skill of Ira Grollman of OMKT Disc Services and Jeff Root made for a fine recording in a difficult venue. In addition I'd like to thank Steve Gaetz and Jeff Vaghini of Bedlam-Sound for their contributions.

The only songs not recorded live that night were the opening song "Come Journey With Me" which was recorded later at The Root Cellar, and "She Appeared To Be 18 or 19 years Old," which I recorded on a handheld camcorder and that Jeff Root mastered for me later. I also added a few vocal harmonies in the studio after the fact.

What an amazing musical and creative journey this has been!

POSTCRIPT

THE MIGHTY MUSE AND THE IMPORTANCE OF SONG IN THE 21ST CENTURY
By Jon McAuliffe

How come one person can write a song and another can't? Is there some trick involved, some educational source one can pursue or some special knowledge one can acquire to write songs that move the heart and soul of the world? Yes, and no. Mostly no. Simply put, songwriting is a gift. Some people have that gift and some don't. Sure. You CAN take songwriting courses that teach the rudiments of songwriting and learn how to get those creative juices flowing.

There are also hundreds of books out there on the subject and some of them might even help. Once you figure out how to tap the inner source, how to make the gift breathe, how to get the ball rolling that gets you into the zone that all accomplished songwriters must inhabit in order to turn the raw materials of inspiration into a song that will move a listener, from there the process begins IF you have the gift. The gift is essential and no amount of inner manipulation or outer study can make that happen. So where does this gift come from and how can you get it to come your way? Numerous opinions have been promulgated to answer this question and the answer is simply that no one really knows. Thousands of songwriters have responded to the question and most seem to agree on one thing. The songs are there before the songwriter hears them internally. Bob Dylan once said something like "Nobody really writes a song. God writes the songs. Any song I've ever "written" was already there before I heard it in my head."

I just happened to be in the right place at the right time to hear and receive it and it either came to me pretty much fully realized or I coaxed it out over time. That's pretty much the universal response. Songwriters often talk about working on certain songs for years, polishing lines, working on the bridge, perfecting a chorus, manipulating the melody to get it to a place where it perfectly supports a lyric. But some of the best and most successful songs ever written came inside of 30 minutes, fully shaped melodically with the lyrics seemingly falling out of the air onto the songwriter's legal pad. Sometimes it's as easy as flipping a switch. Other times the process seems to take forever. There is a muse involved in this process and it's not clear how it chooses to dispense its gifts, nor to whom. Once the songwriter has discovered whether or not he or she has this gift, then the real work begins. More often than not it is the songwriter who determines whether or not they've written something worthy of a listener's time, and strong enough to move that listener on an emotional level. Sometimes the songwriter knows instantly that they've been given a song that speaks for them personally or speaks for larger segment of people universally. Those are the greatest moments the songwriter can experience. That first realization that one possesses a song of maximum impact is greater than performing that song on stage for an appreciative audience. Of course, the songwriter can be wrong, too. It's easy to think one has something that's perfect, only to realize a month or so later that it's a dud. But there are some litmus tests. Singer/Songwriter Bob Franke has said that "If when you begin writing a song, and that song makes you weep, chances are it will do the same to the listener and chances also are that you're on to something strong when it initially moves you like that." And most songwriters will agree that some songs just seem to come out of nowhere and are pure joy to write and sing over and over again; usually, the joy of singing them is infectious on a wide level. Think of "Bang On The Drum" by Todd Rundgren. Songs have emotional release points that send us sky high or disturb our souls with irrefutable truths that make us remember pain or sorrow or joy or gain or loss, that connect us to the rest of the human race by dint of shared experience.

There are all kinds of songs. Good ones, bad ones, average ones and the rarer kind—standards; songs that speak for major segments of humanity because they speak to the deepest part of the human experience. Songs like "What Is This Thing Called Love?" or "Night And Day" (Cole Porter); "Blowin' In The Wind" or "Every Grain of Sand" (Bob Dylan); "If You Could Read My Mind" (Gordon Lightfoot); "Both Sides Now" (Joni Mitchell); "School Day" or "Back In The USA" or "Rock & Roll Music" (Chuck Berry); "Yesterday" (Paul McCartney); "Imagine" (John Lennon); "Danger Zone" (Percy Mayfield); "I'm So Lonesome I Could Cry" (Hank Williams), and thousands more. Great songs inspire our hearts, minds and spirits and are powerful uniters of the human condition.

Given that today's music industry is built more around flash, fashion, dance or surface glitz than any kind of measurable quality of songwriting, one may have to search more diligently today to hear great songs than one did in the past. Of course, not everyone is moved by a great song or by great songwriting, per se. Some, like those teens of 50 years ago on Dick Clark's American Bandstand, simply prefer a good beat so they can dance to it. For those of us who are moved by great songwriting, however, one might be surprised to learn that many of the best songwriters writing today can be heard right here in the Northeast, if one is willing to seek them out.

Given the marketing paradigm and virtually closed shop mentality affecting creativity today, what Bob Dylan once referred to as "$uckce$$" (why are only well known songs heard on programs like *America's Got Talent* or *American Idol* and not original compositions?), one might have to do more than click on itunes to hear great songs in 2011. Some of the greatest songs being written today are not often heard on radio or readily available in the online marketplace. You have to search them out. The level of quality extant today might have been astonishing to realize 30 or 40 years ago. Some of the best songwriters I've ever heard are offering their work right here, right now in the Northeast at local open mics and various performance venues.

They are not household names but if their work had been heard in the '70s or '80s they quite possibly would have been. Among them are Stuart Ferguson, Lyn-O'Conor Ferguson, Lori Diamond, Jane Fallon, Kim Jennings, Bob Franke, Dan Cloutier, Levi Schmidt, Terence Hegarty, Alan Crane, Mark Stepakoff, Tom Smith, Mally Smith, Oen Kennedy, Robin Batteau, David Buskin, Marc Bridge, Jim Bauer (of the band Dagmar), Steve Howard, Dan Emino, Andy Pratt, Roly Salley, Chris Thompson, Jon Waterman, Ruthann Baler, Lisa Martin, Jim Dawson, Dave Murphy, Jud Caswell, Barbara Keith and more.

There have been epochs in history when great art was produced in nearly every genre, the zeitgeist seemingly sprinkling the muse like a drunken sailor sprinkles money at a bar. The rise of jazz in the 1920s; cubism, Dadaism, surrealism, abstract expressionism, Paris in the 20s; the so-called "Swing" era; Bebop; the literary revolution of the '20s that found new expression and broke down the walls of conformity by the 1950s in the so-called Beat Generation, rhythm & blues in the late 1940s, the coalescence over three decades of original country music, rockabilly, rock & roll, the so-called "folk revival" of the late 1950s into the 1960s, folk rock; the British Invasion, the singer-songwriter movement and more. Those eras seemed to explode as if something magical had been released into the mainstream by a minority of artists who had their finger on the pulse of something mystical. Might it be that such a renaissance is underway now that has yet to come to full fruition or simply be understood for what it is? GREAT songs are indeed being written in our midst.

© 2010, Jon McAuliffe. Used by permission
Find the complete blogpost at
http://www.jonmcauliffe.com/index.php/blog

SELECTED BIBLIOGRAPHY

Cook, Sylvia Jenkins. From Tobacco Road to Route 66: The Southern Poor White in Fiction. Chapel Hill, NC: University of North Carolina Press, 1976. Questia. Web. 17 Feb. 2011.

DuVell, Leland. Arkansas: Colony and State. Little Rock Rose Publishing Co, 1973. Quoted in Ashmore, Harry. Arkansas History, WW Norton, NY, 1978.
.
Gregory, James N. The Southern Diaspora: How the Great Migrations of Black and White Southerners Transformed America. Chapel Hill, NC: University of North Carolina Press, 2005. Questia. Web. 17 Feb.2011.

Johnson III, Ben F. Arkansas in Modern America 1930 – 1999. University of Arkansas Press, 2000.

Klein, Joe. Woody Guthrie: A Life. New York, NY: Alfred A. Knopf, 1999.

McDonough, Nancy. Garden Sass: A Catalog of Arkansas. Folkways. Coward, McCann, and Geoghan, 1975.

McGovern, James R. <u>And a Time for Hope: Americans in the Great Depression</u>. Westport, CT: Praeger, 2000. Questia.Web. 17 Feb. 2011.

Steinbeck, John. <u>The Grapes of Wrath</u>. New York: Penguin, 2002.

Wilkinson, Alec. <u>The Protest Singer</u>. New York, NY: Alfred A. Knopf, 2009.

Song Lyric Credits:
"Highways and Heartaches" Joe Ely
"Bookends" Paul Simon

Additional Resources:
www.amadorgold.net
www.oldstatehouse.com
www.openwriting.com/archives/2006/11/old_brush_arbor_1.php
www.gendisasters.com/data1/or/fires/silverlake-firedec1894.htm
www.historylink.org/index.cfm?DisplayPage=output.cfm&file_id=317
4cknowledgements.

JANE ROSS FALLON began her career singing in a trio with her sister and cousin. Later she received formal vocal training at Eastern Oregon University and spent several years in local musical theater.

She is also an award winning songwriter with five CD's of original music to her credit. Her songs have been played on radio stations throughout the world.

A veteran performer, Fallon is known for her smooth, rich voice and well-written songs. With vocals that have been called "angelic" and "mesmerizing" by Boston's Metronome magazine, her original songs "combine humor, intelligence, and deep musicality with an artfulness that is unusual." (Wildy Haskell, www.wildysworld.com). Her newest CD "Gemini Rising", co-produced with Jeff Root and Jim Henry, has been called by Jay Whelan of www. rambles.net " a collection of songs that stitches itself together note by note and warms the soul." Bill Copeland (www.billcopelandmusic new.com) calls her writing "beautiful, honest, and powerful."

She lives in New Hampshire with her husband, Jack, where she teaches Composition and Communications at Southern New Hampshire University and is the mother of three wonderful human beings named Theresa, Patrick, and Nicholas.

Made in the USA
Columbia, SC
20 July 2018